Newfie Therapy
Coloring Book

Lisa Schiller

Copyright 2020 TimberKnolls Spirit Cove, Inc.

All rights reserved

No part of this book may be reproduced, or stored in a retrieval system, or transmitted in any form or by any means, electronic, mechanical, photocopying, recording, or otherwise, without express written permission of the publisher.

ISBN: 9798665016863

Created by: Lisa Schiller
Cover design & Illustrations by: Holly Mitchell
Back Cover Images: Holly Bloom-Ranieri
Photographers: Benita Edds, Patti Sutherland, Kajal Schiller

All rights reserved

No part of this book may be reproduced, or stored in a retrieval system, or transmitted in any form or by any means, electronic, mechanical, photocopying, recording, or otherwise, without express written permission of the publisher.

ISBN-13: 9798665016863

Created by: Lisa Schiller
Cover design & Illustrations by: Holly Mitchell
Back Cover Images: Holly Bloom-Ranieri
Photographers: Benita Edds, Patti Sutherland, Kajal Schiller

Printed in the United States of America

Although the author and publisher have made every effort to ensure that the information in this book was correct at press time, the author and publisher do not assume and hereby disclaim any liability to any party for any loss, damage, or disruption caused by errors or omissions, whether such errors or omissions result from negligence, accident, or any other cause.

TimberKnoll's Spirit Cove is committed to publishing works that are uplifting and spread kindness, hope, and love.
In that spirit, we have published this coloring book.

Printed in the United States of America

In Memory of Hudson, Tess, Oscar, Boone, Landon, Ellie, Sydnee & Greyson.

They transformed lives with their gentle and loving spirits and the light of their souls guide us forward in service to those who need healing.

For their parents, Benita and Patti, whose patience in training was the foundation of their special work. They knew in their hearts; the world needed the comfort and unconditional love of their magnificent, TimberKnoll Newfoundland dogs.

This Coloring book supports Newfoundland Dog Pet Therapy

TimberKnolls Spirit Cove is a 501(c)3 nonprofit organization that provides Newfoundland dog pet therapy to first responders, veterans/military families, seriously ill patients & the medical staff who care for them.

In response to Covid-19 and the increased anxiety it has created, we will be distributing this coloring book to first responders and medical staff who put their lives on the line in service to their communities.

There is a growing need for stress relief from pet therapy, and this is one of the creative and safe, virtual solutions we've identified that could help spread joy through the calming distraction of simple, color therapy.
The Newfoundland dog images on the following pages bring the spirit of these gentle giants where they're needed most.

With your help and contributions, we'll be able to help these special heroes find a little bit of peace in their otherwise chaotic days.

For more information on how you can help make a difference through pet therapy, visit us at:

NewfieTherapy.or or by email: info@newfietherapy.org

Creative Contributions

This coloring book would not be possible without the help of:

Cover Design & Illustration by Holly Mitchell
Back Cover Illustration by Holly Bloom-Ranieri

Photographs by:
Benita Edds, Patti Sutherland
and Kajal Schiller

Newfie Pictures donated by:
Connie Sovie
Mary Braatan
Ken & Hilary Bias
Jana Rife
Katie Marlowe

And of course, special thanks to our beloved Newfies
who had no problem posing for pictures
in return for the occasional cookie.

Newfie Therapy

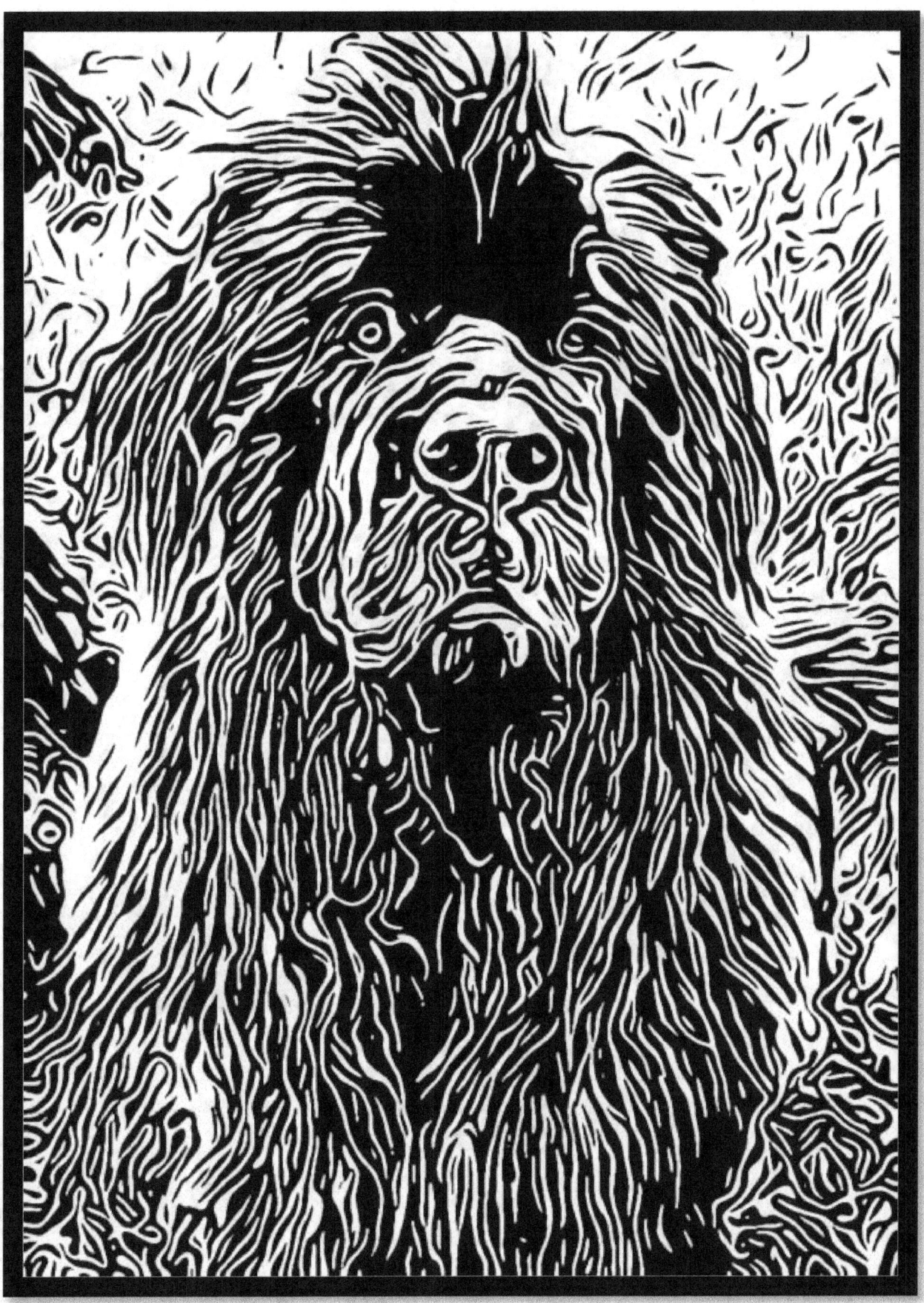

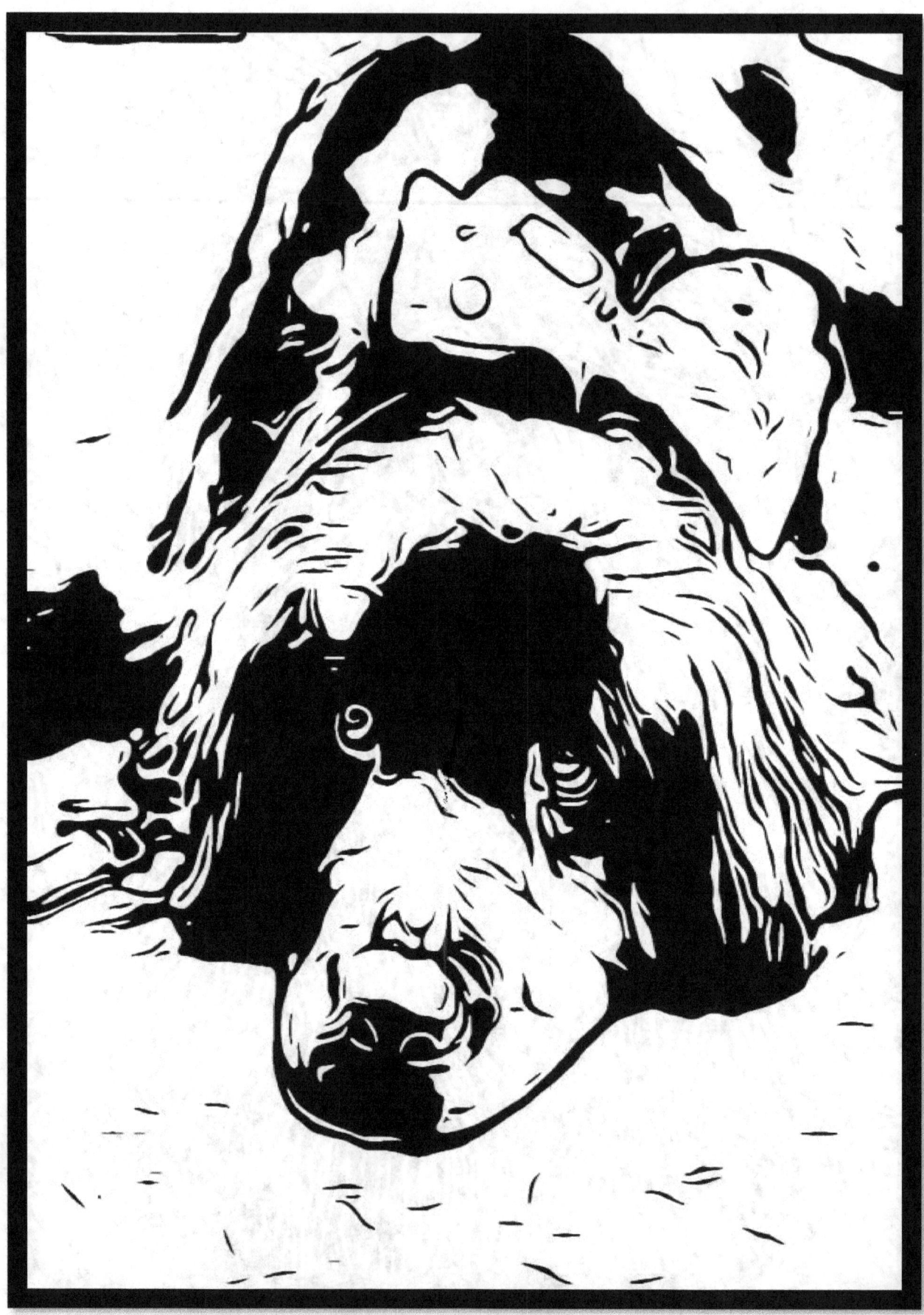

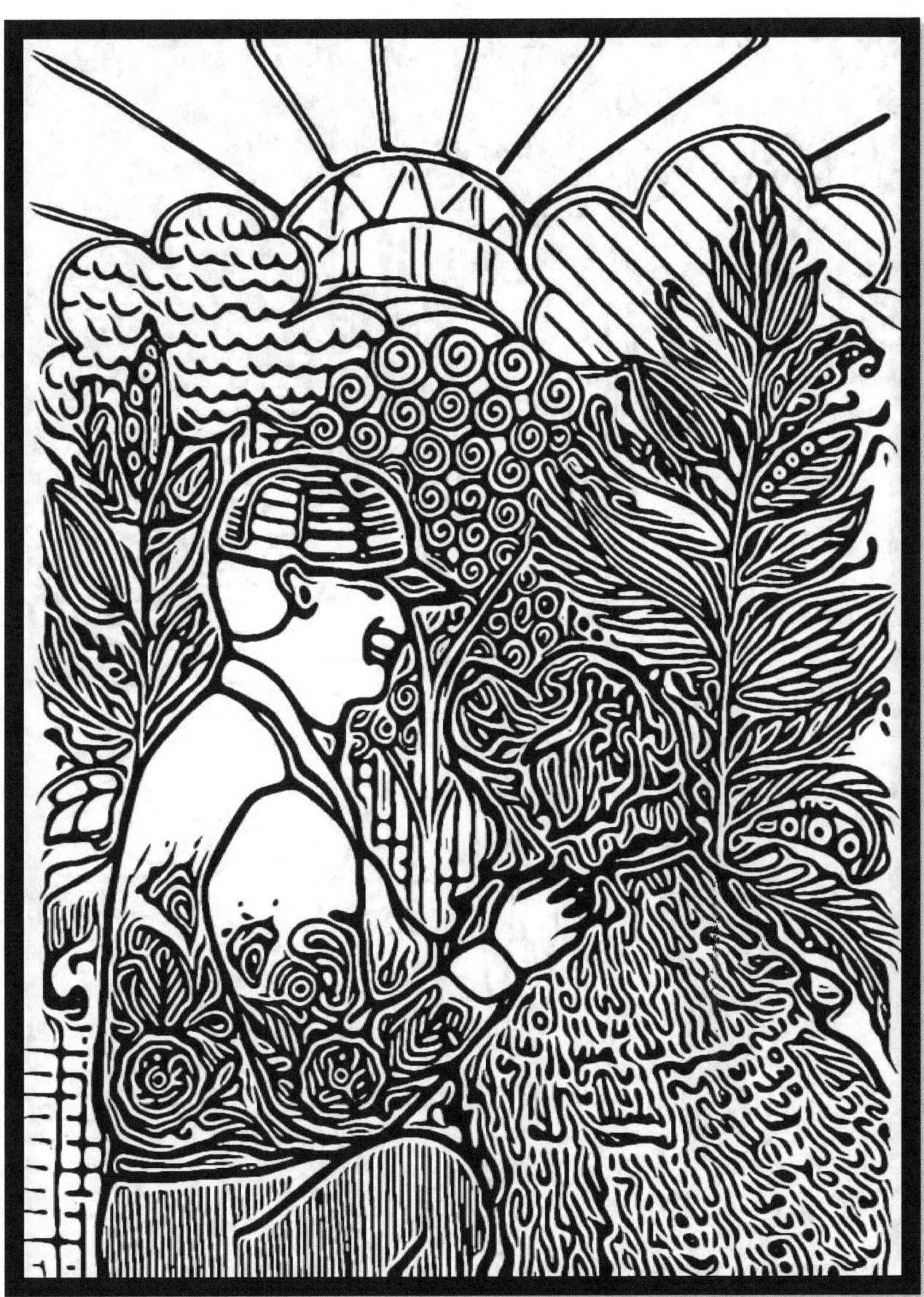

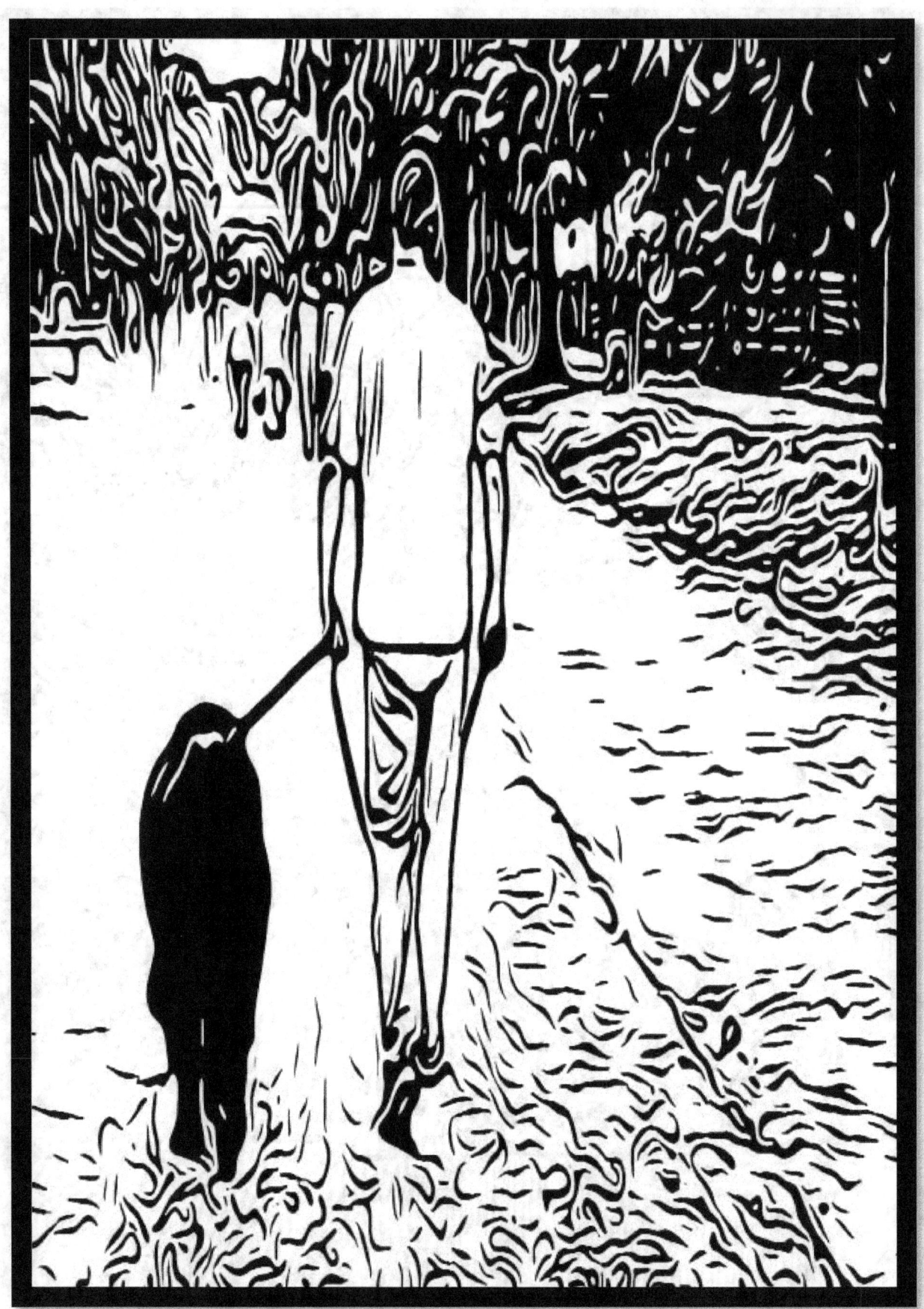

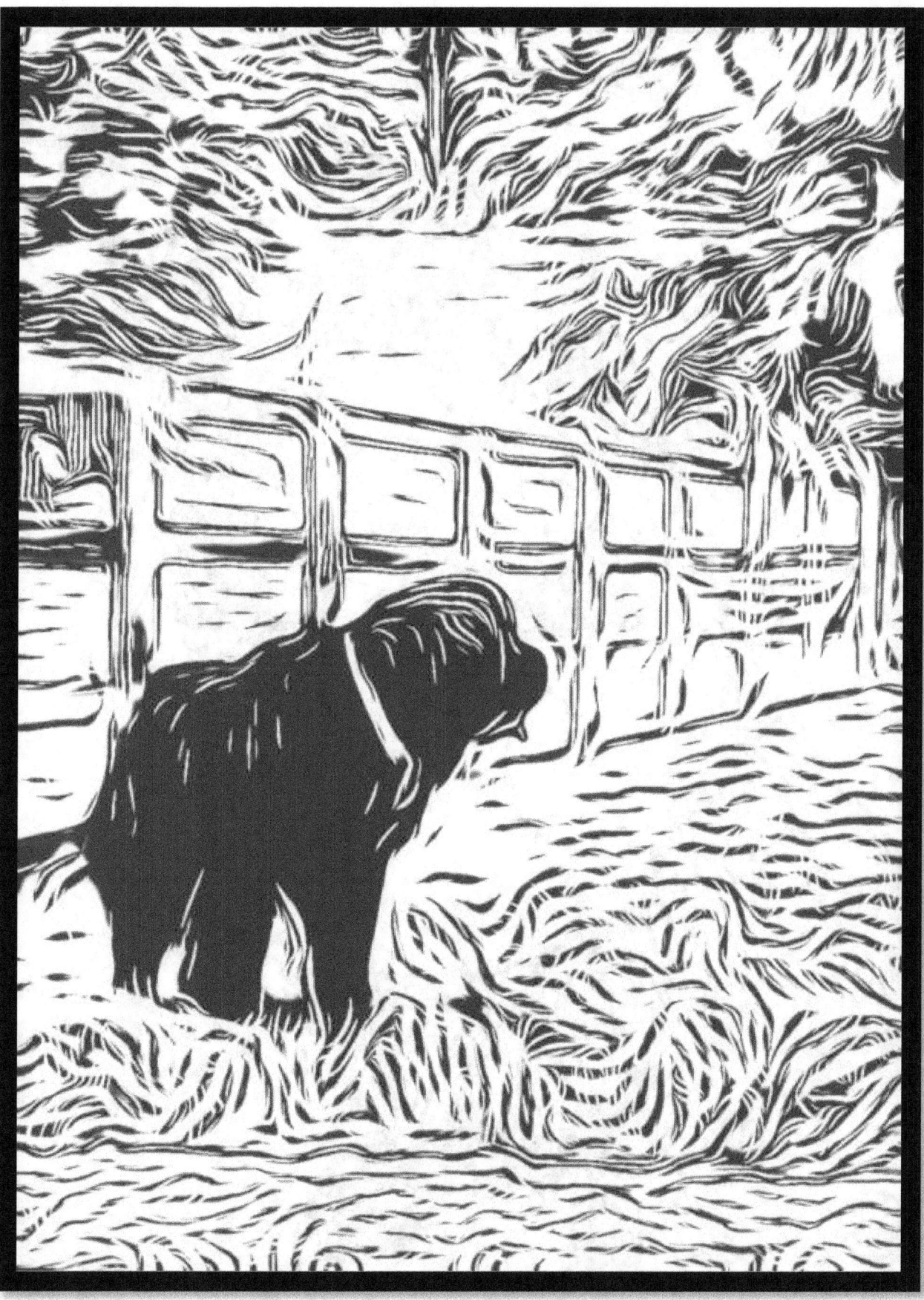

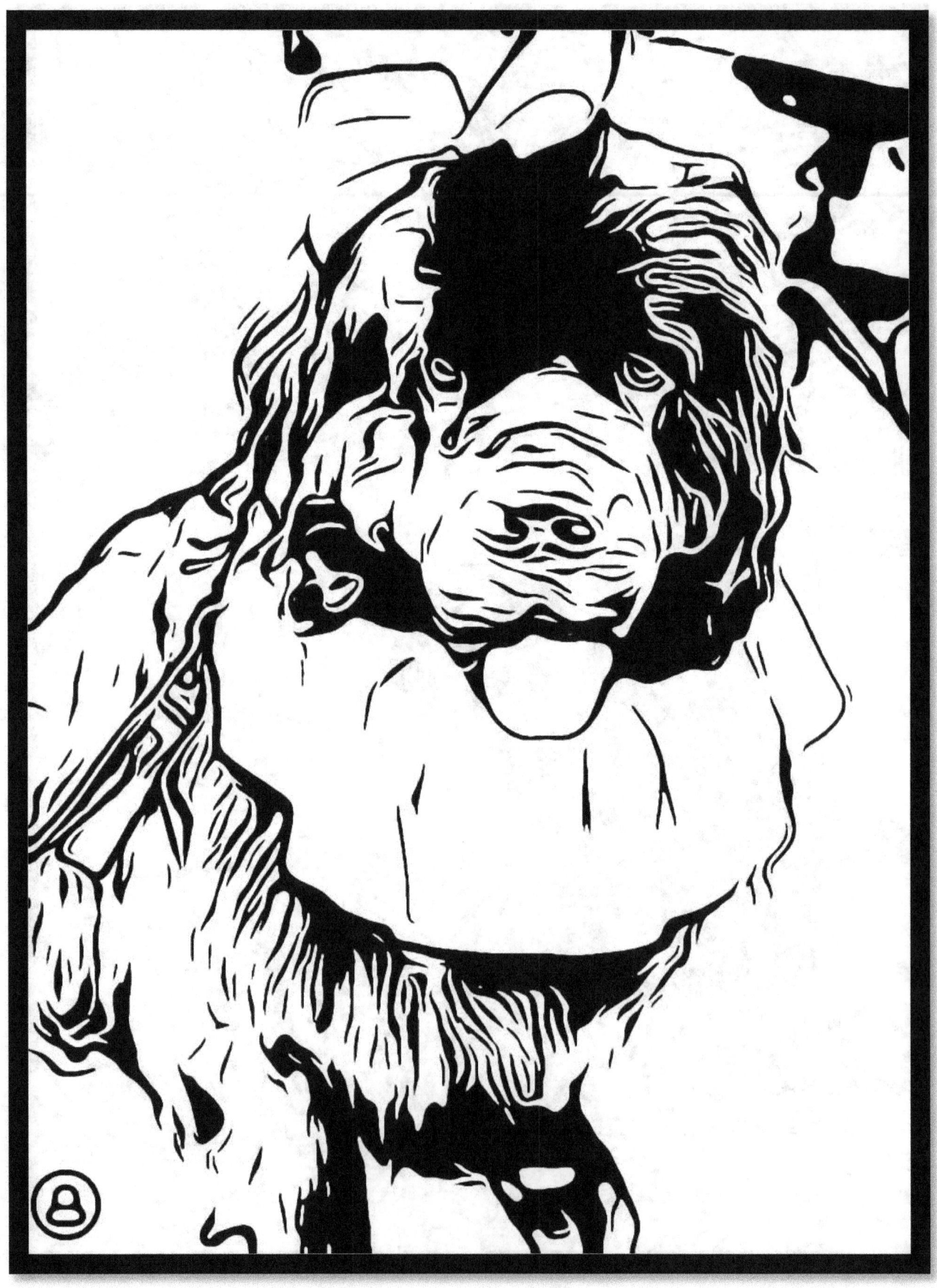

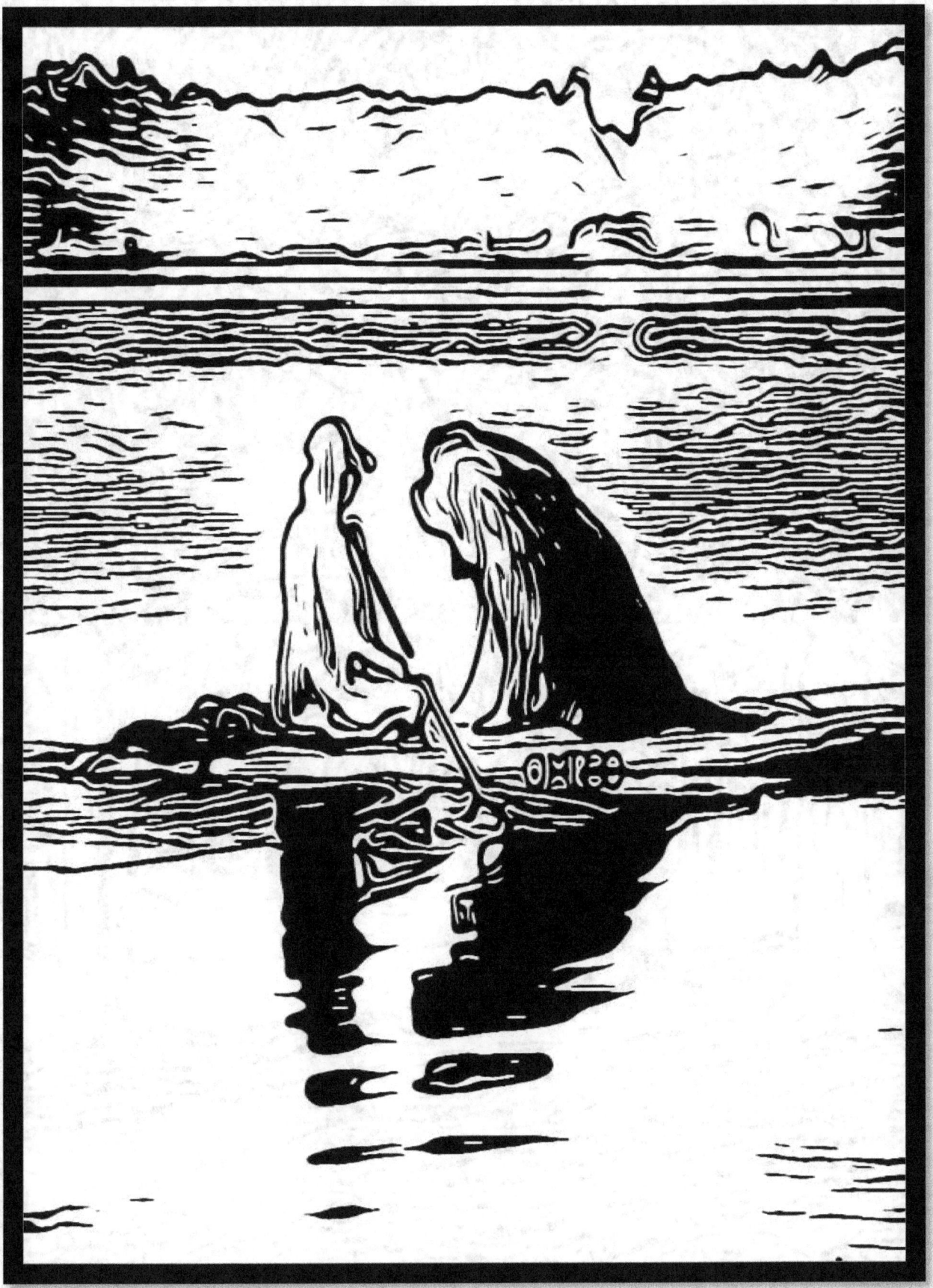

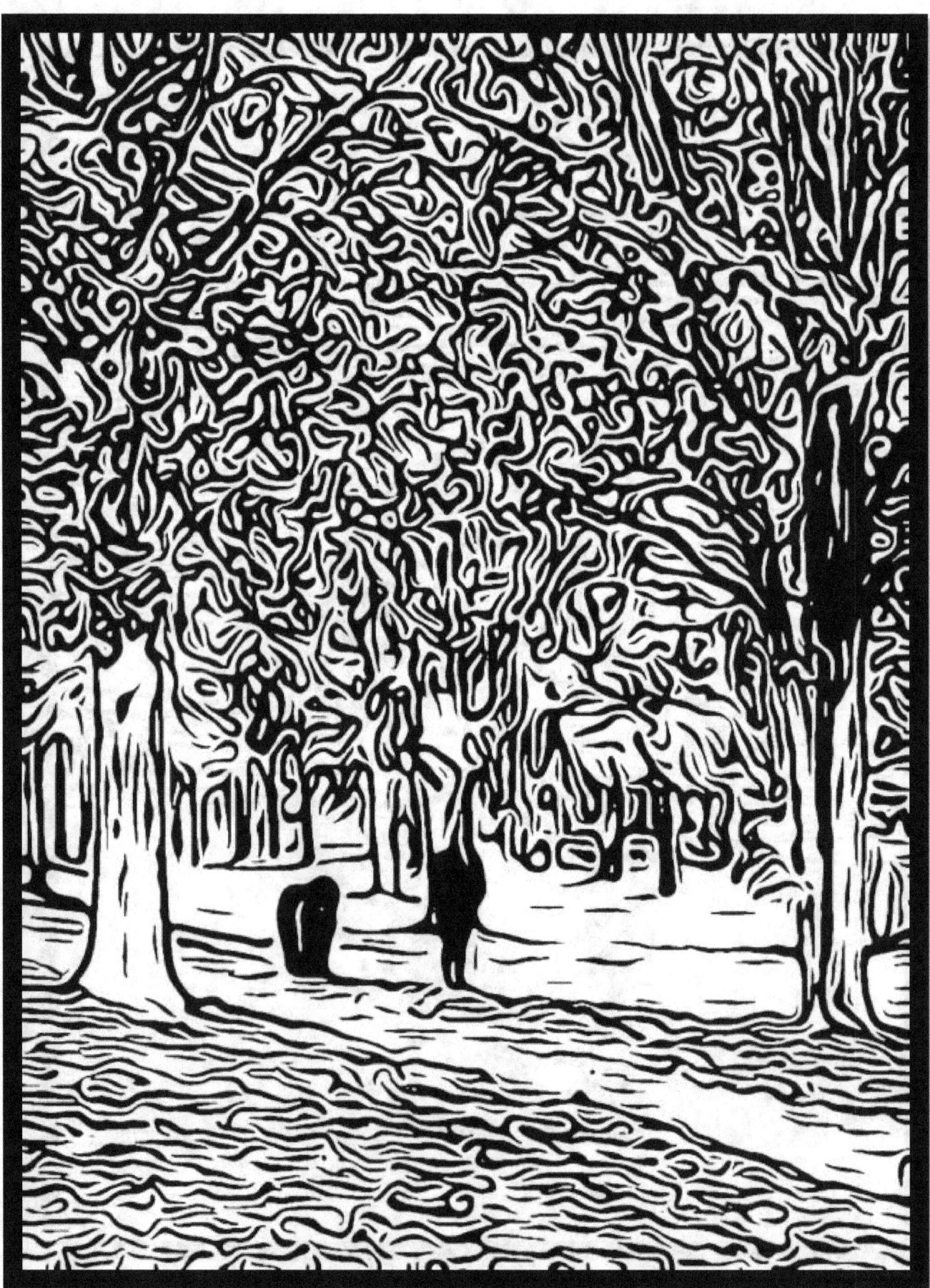

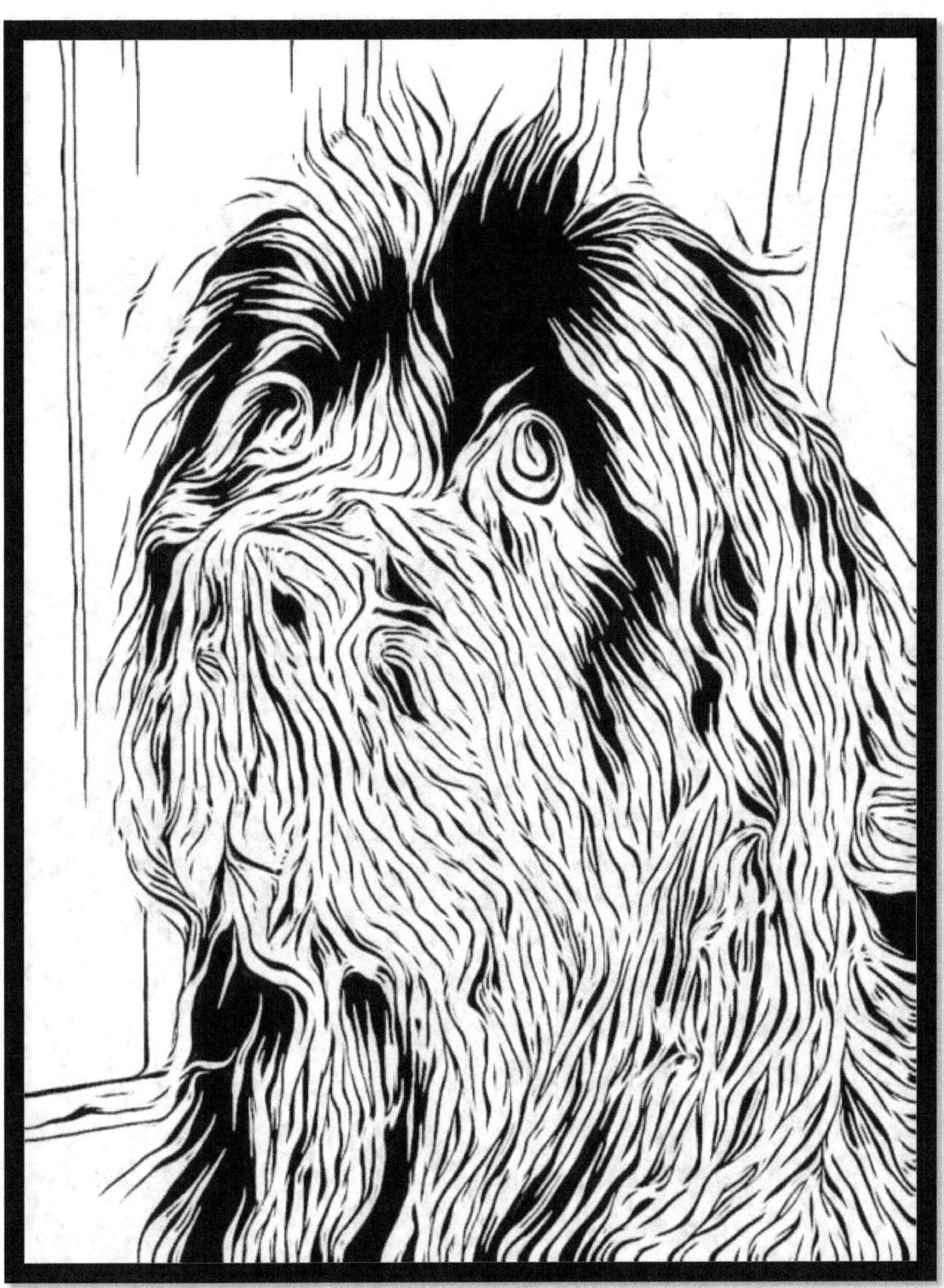

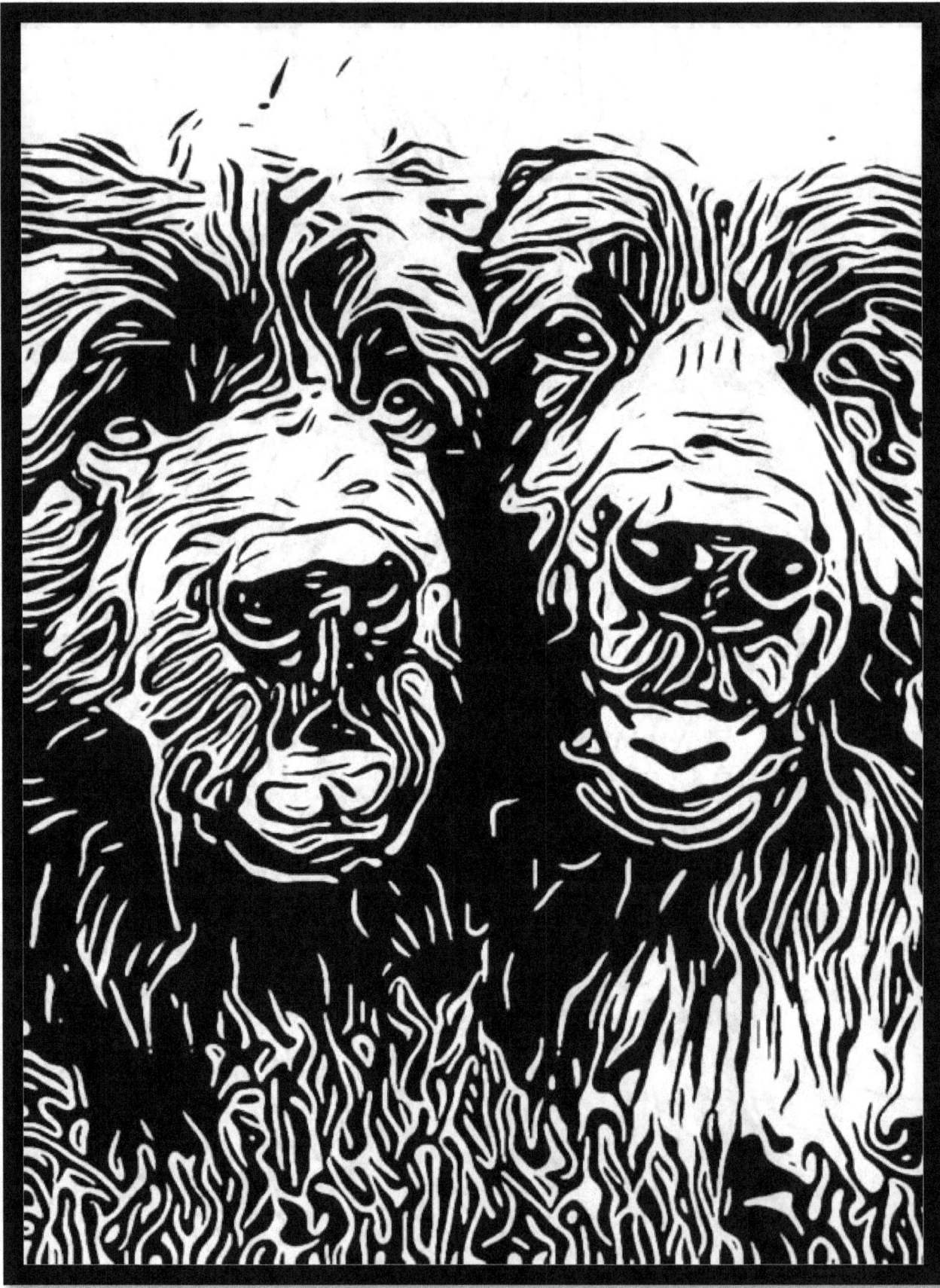

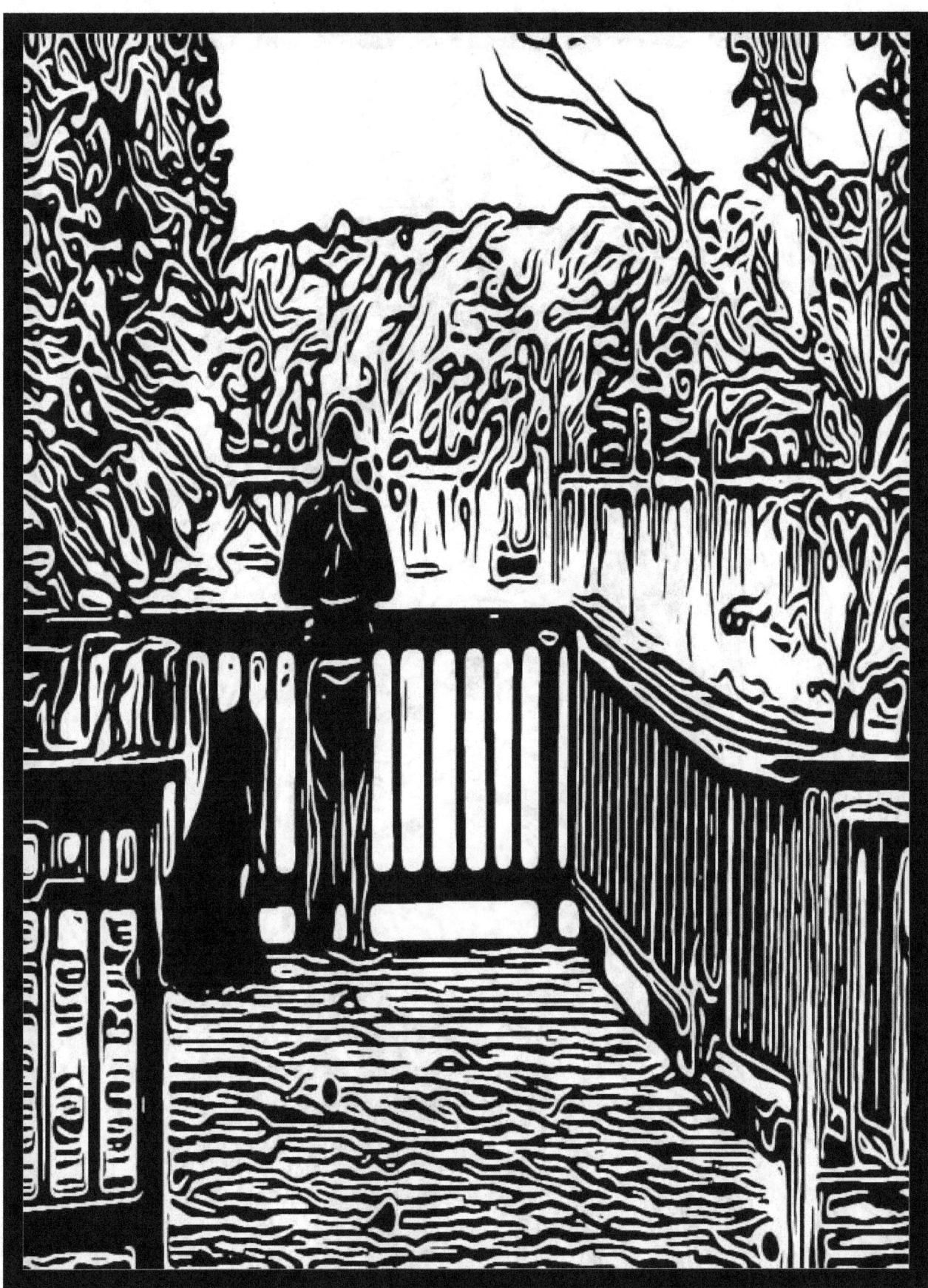

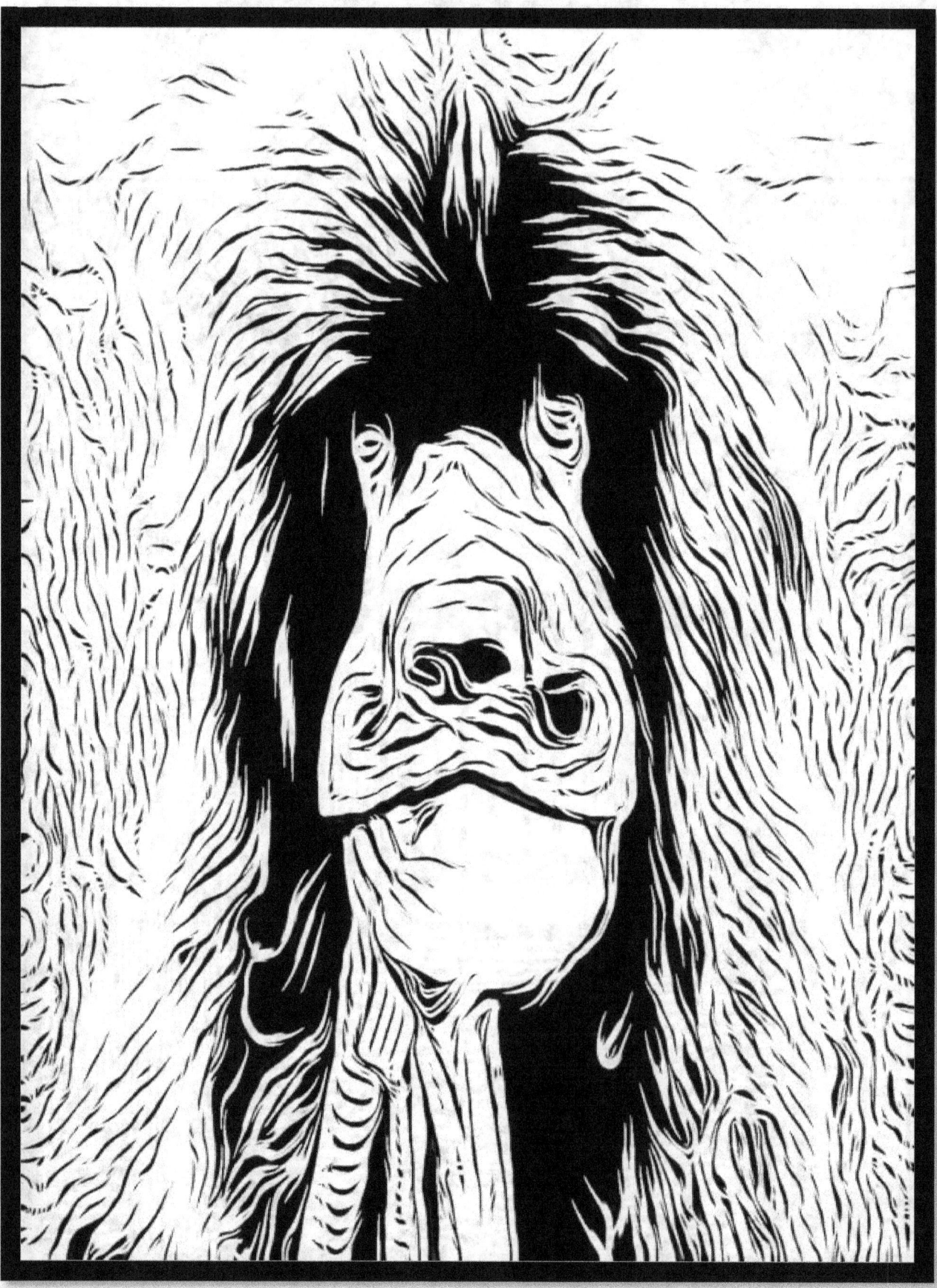

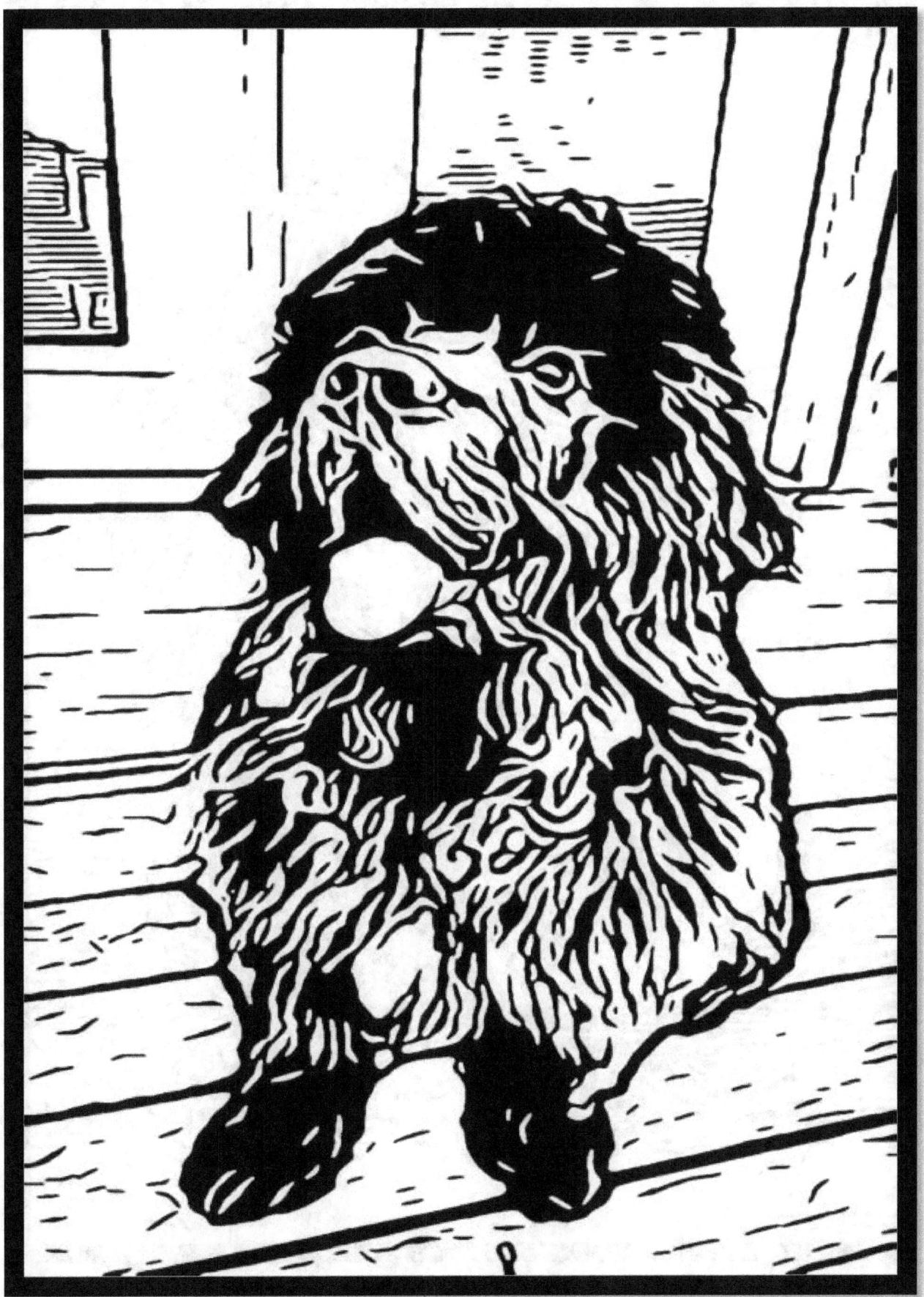

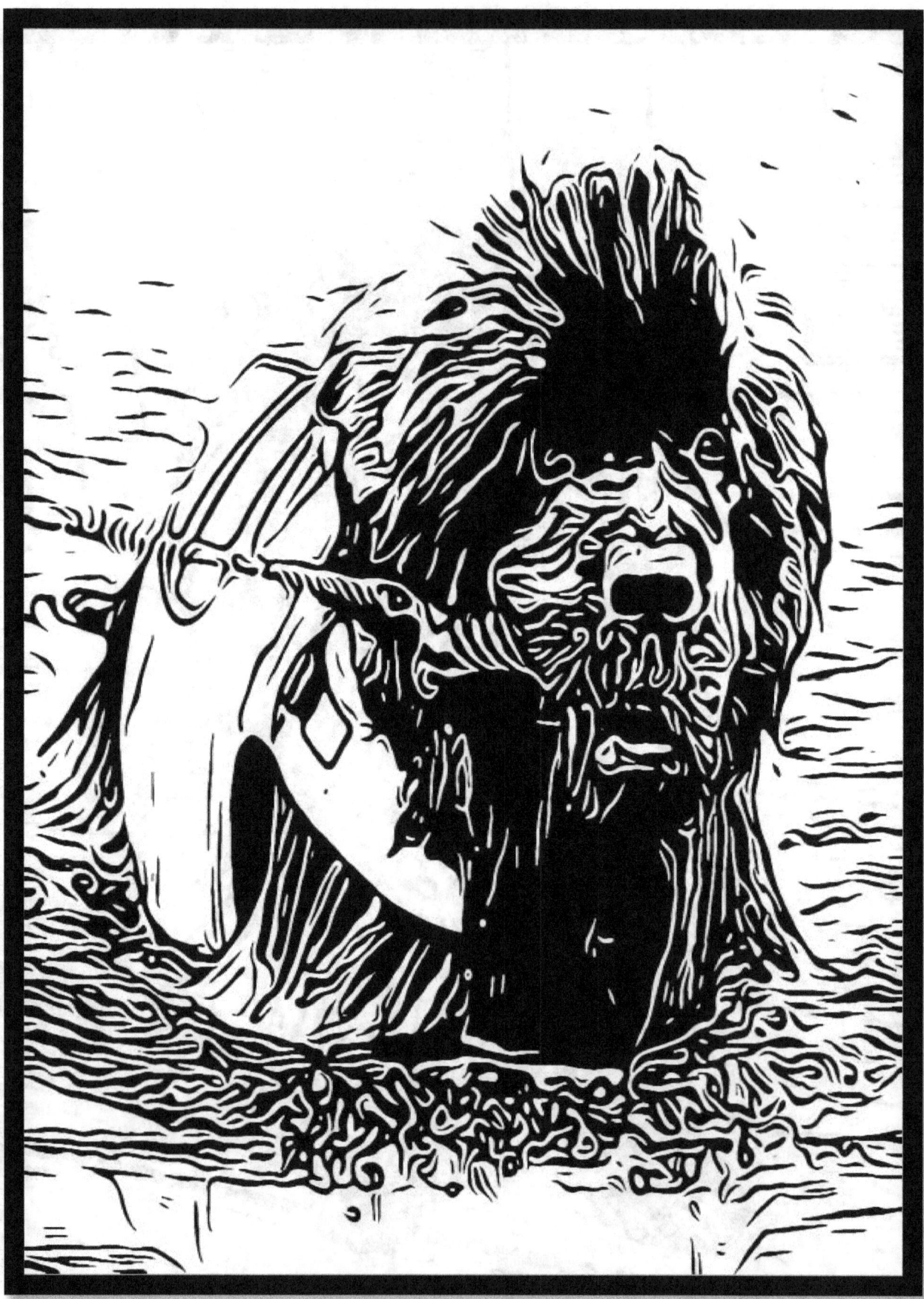

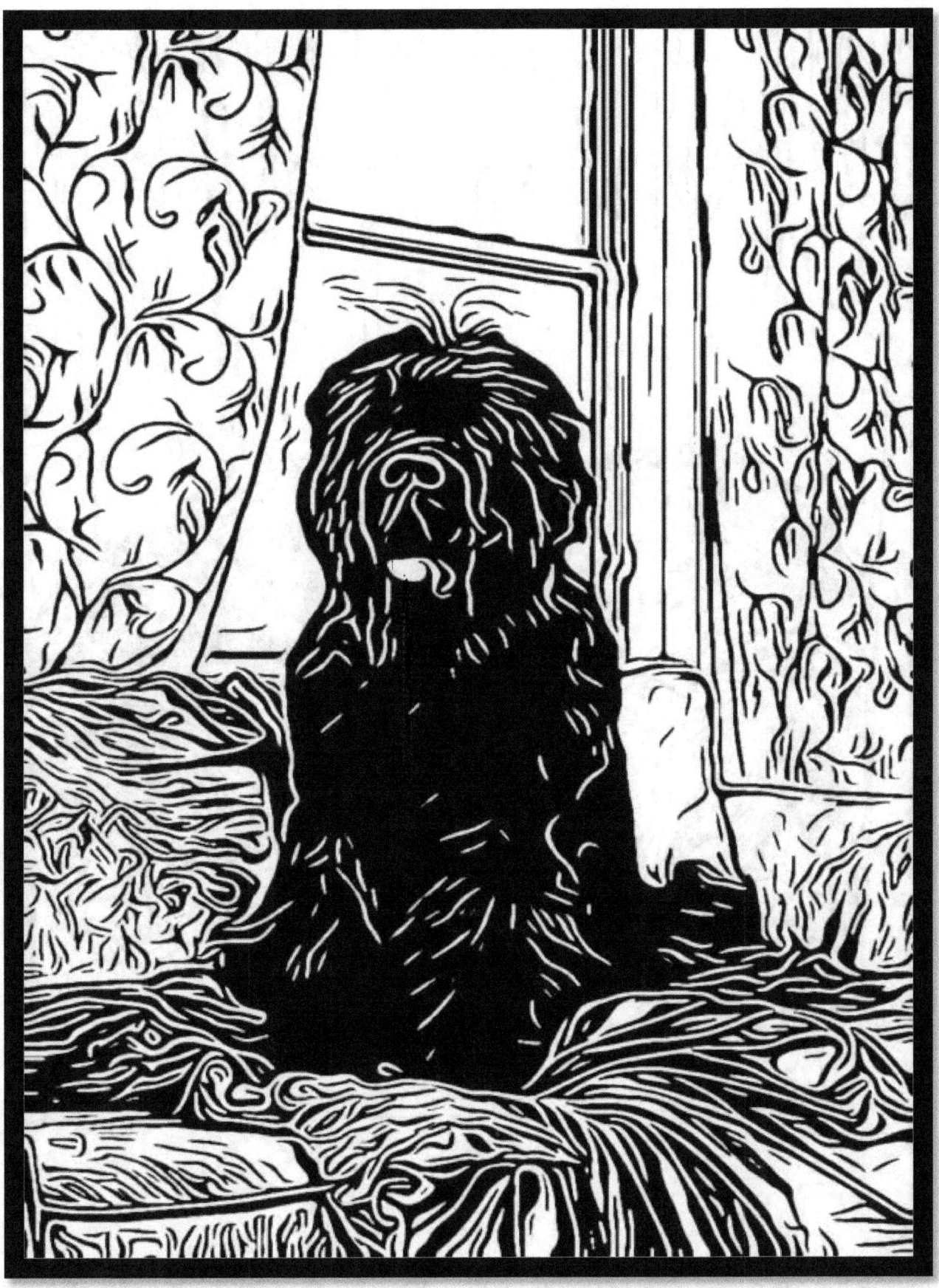

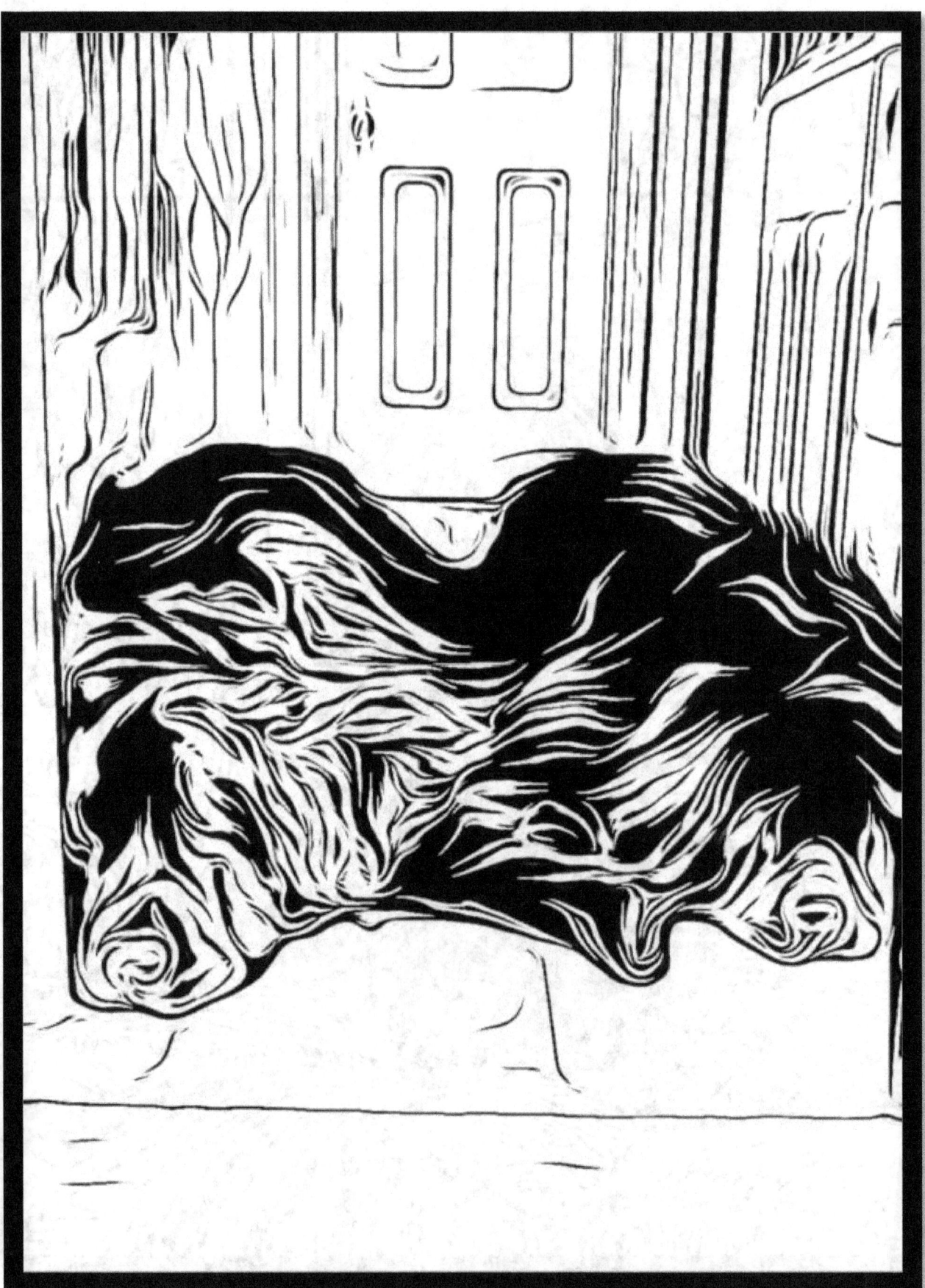

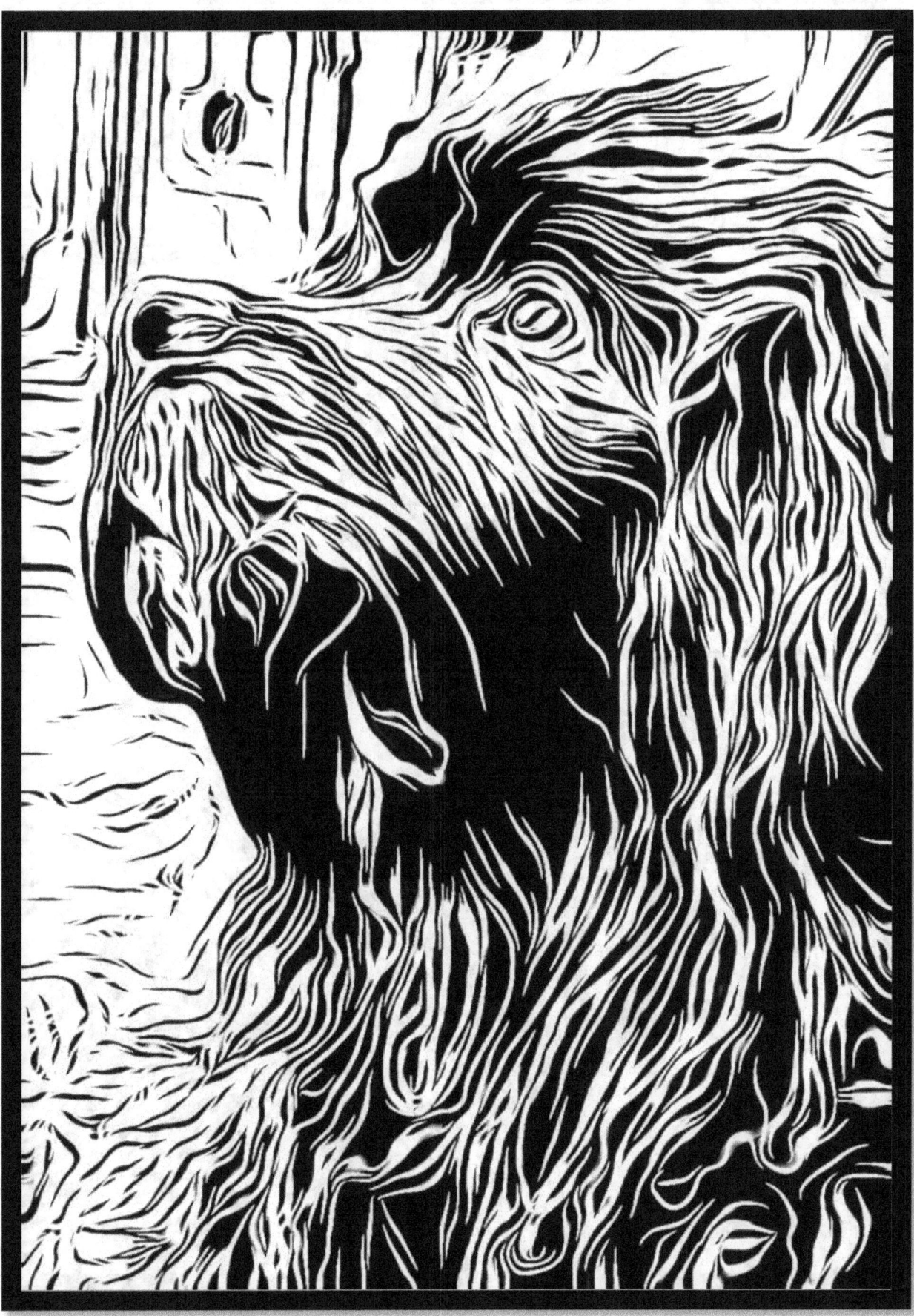

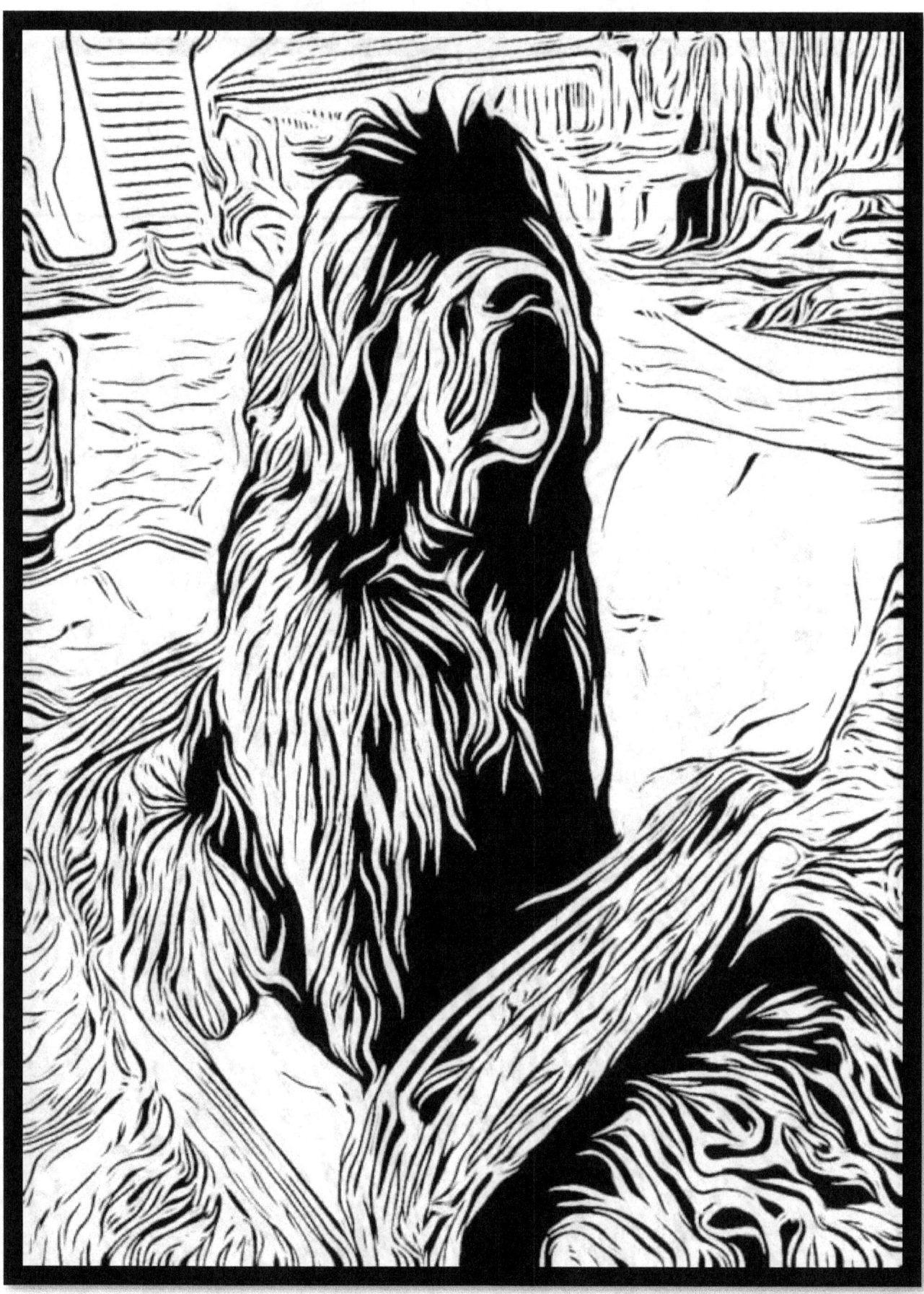

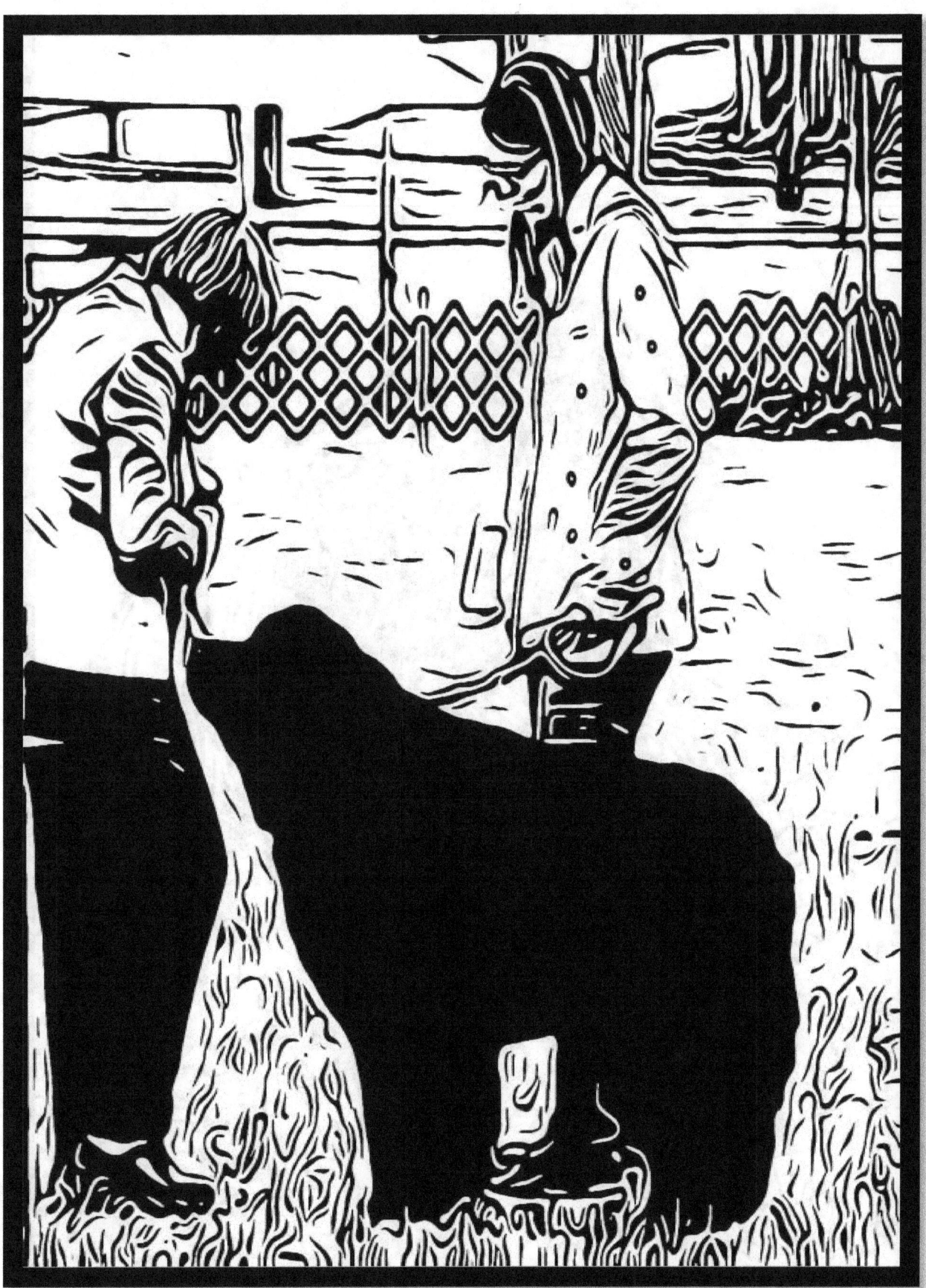

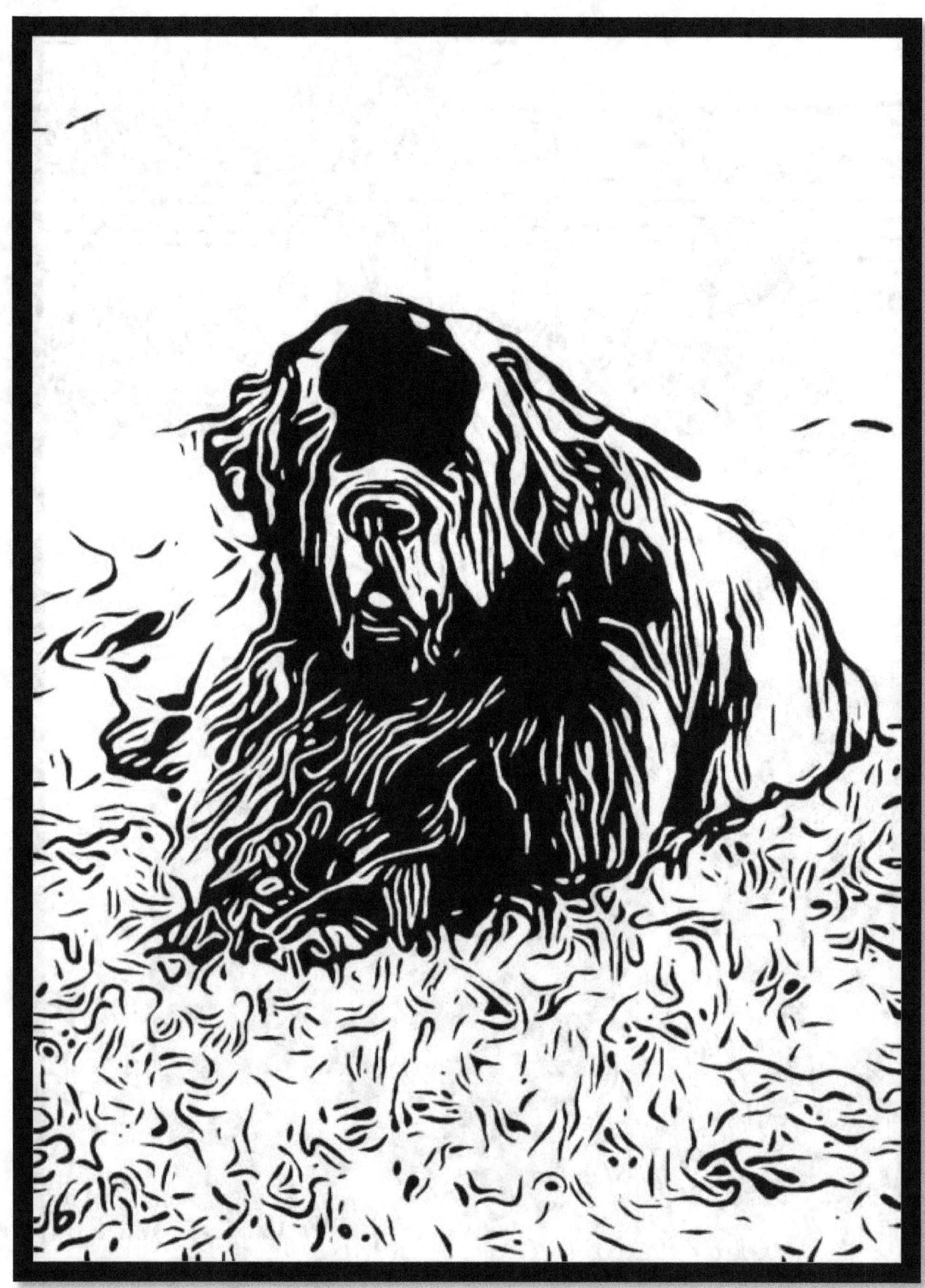

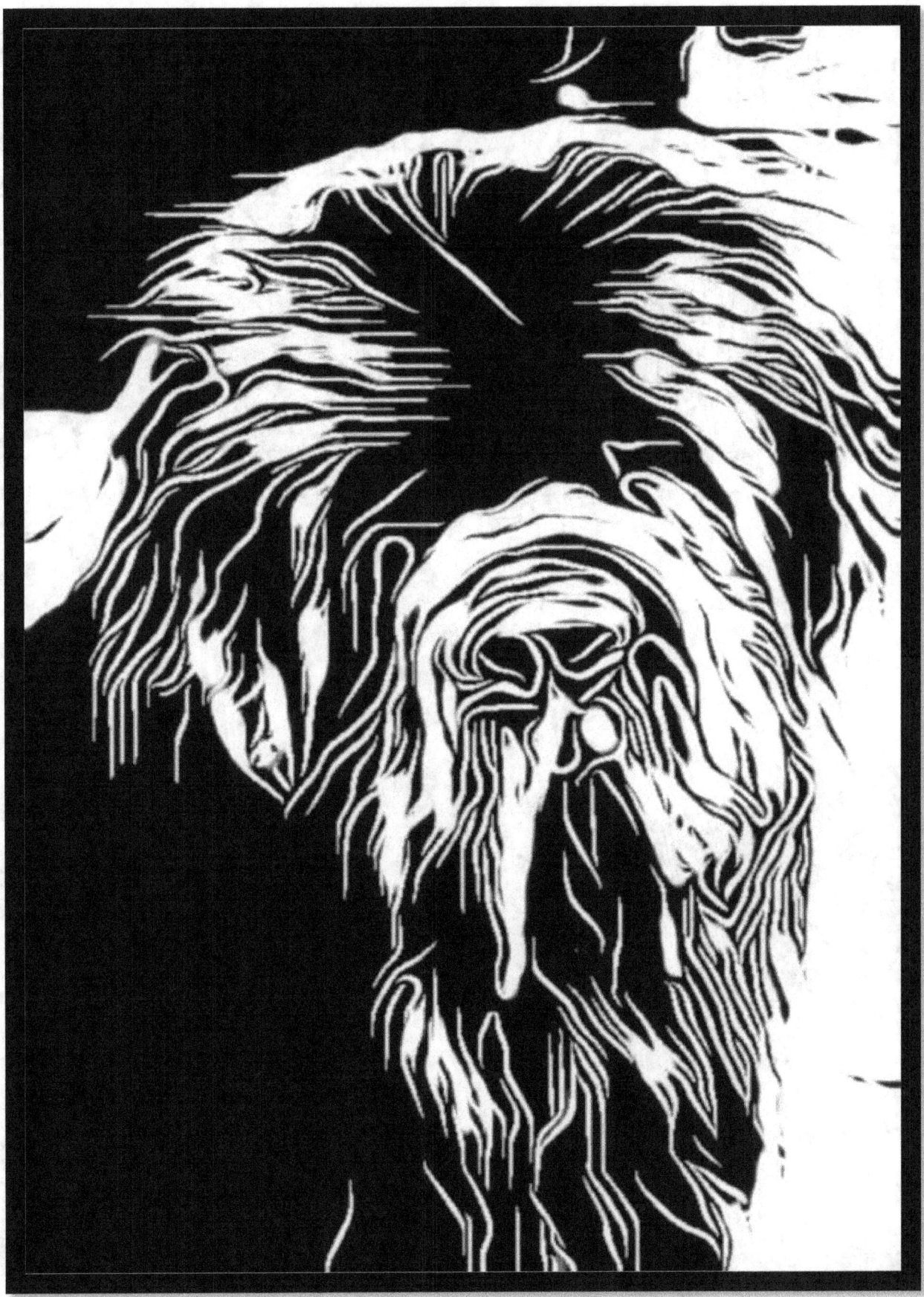

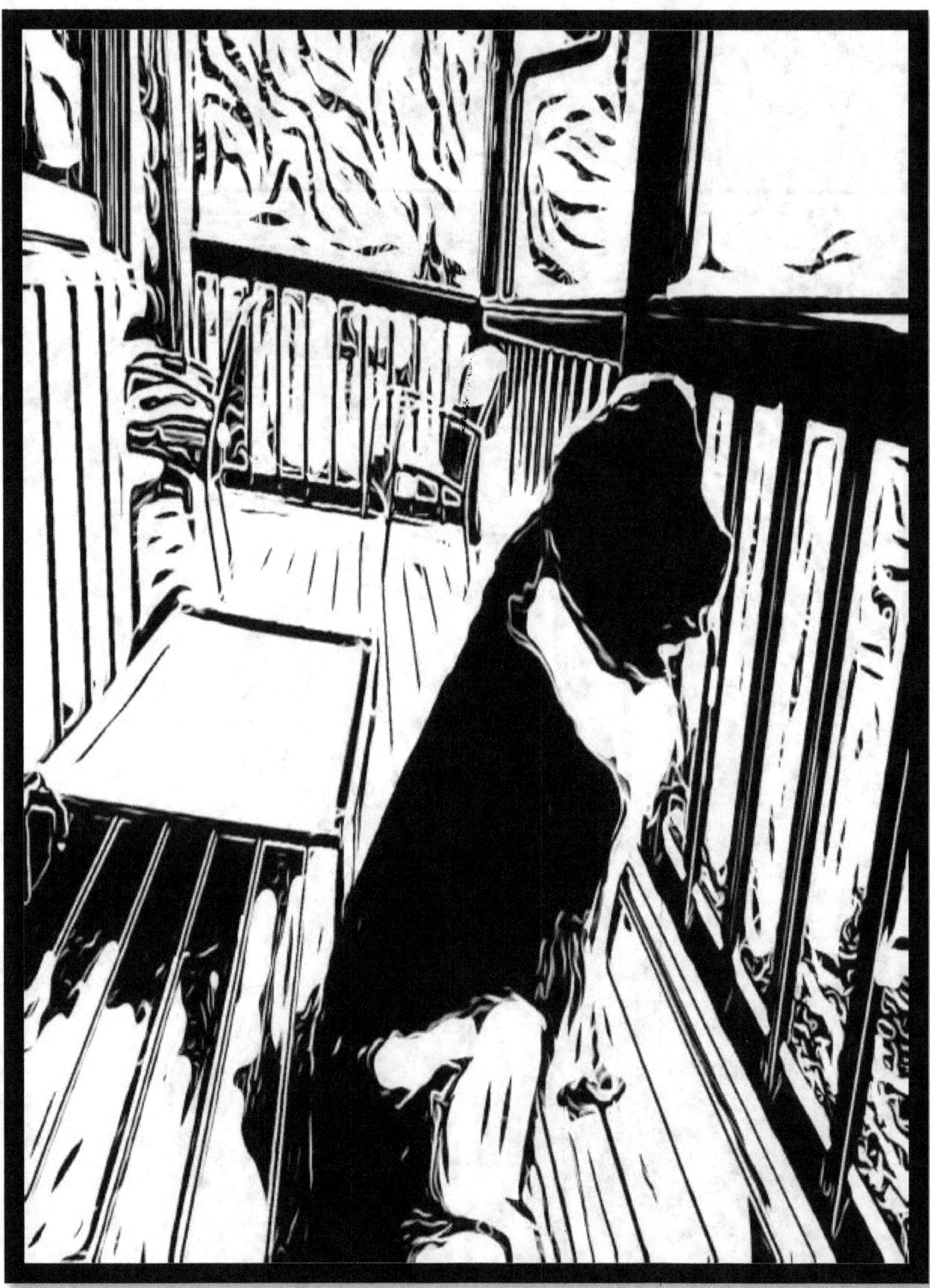

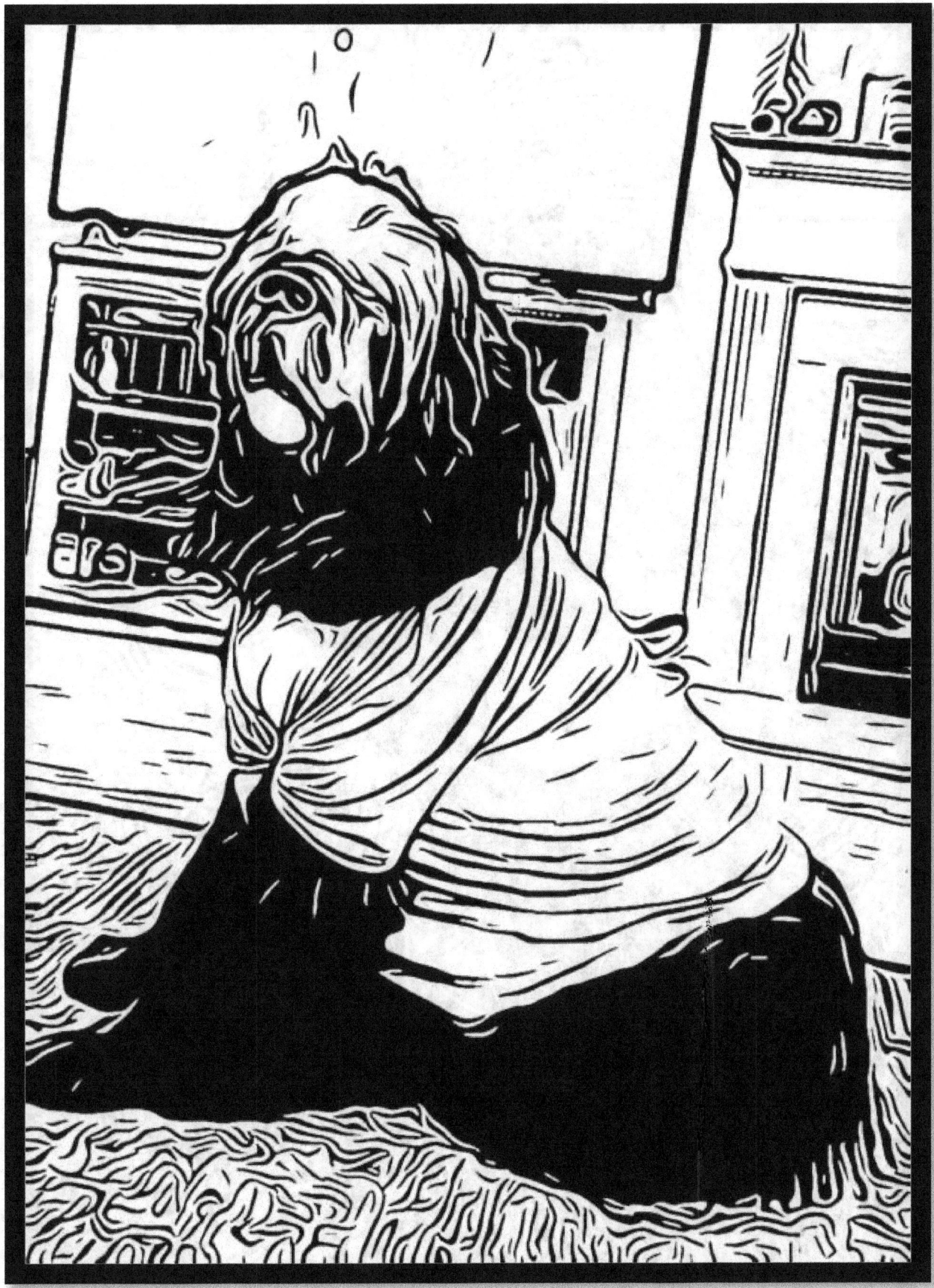

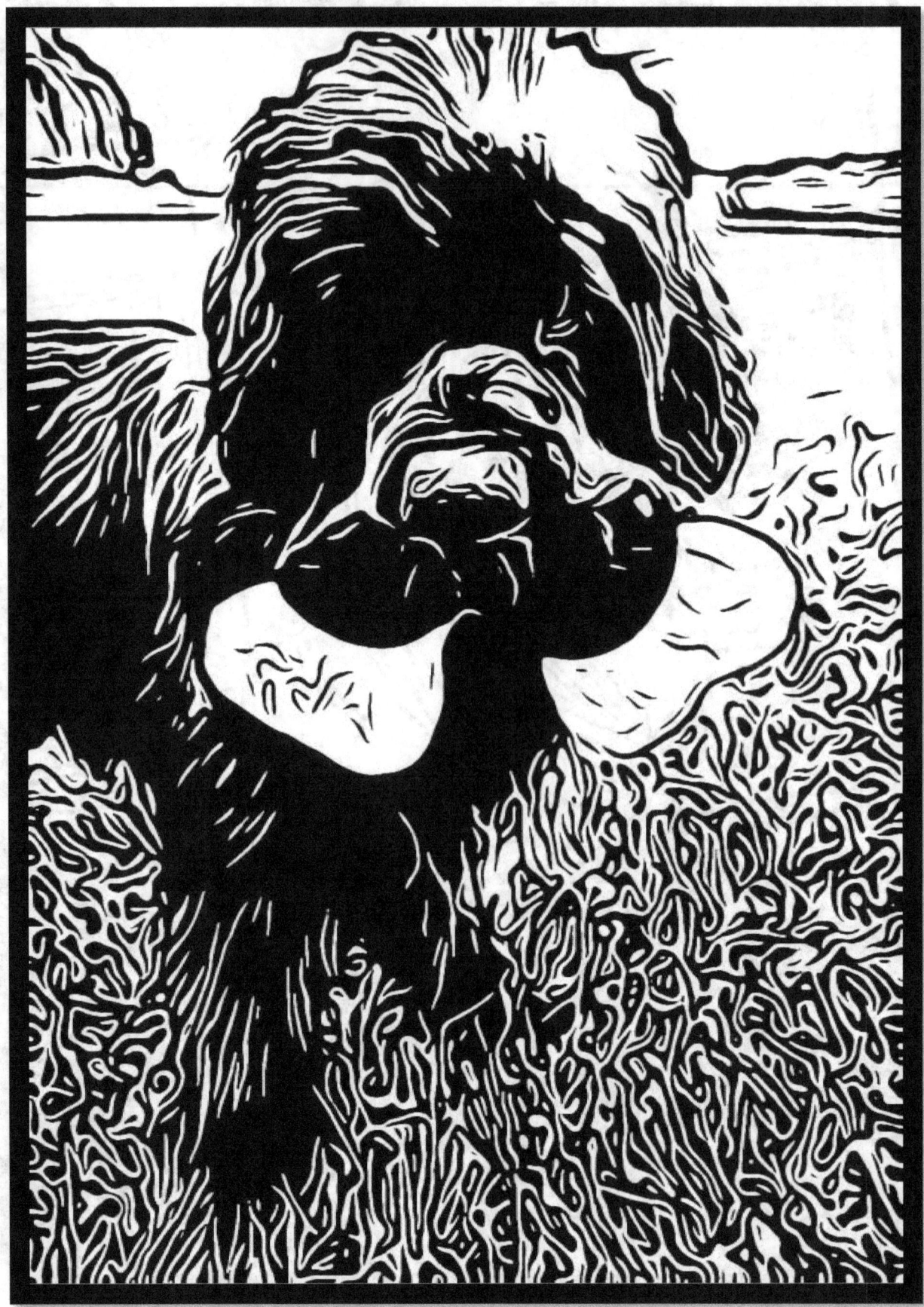

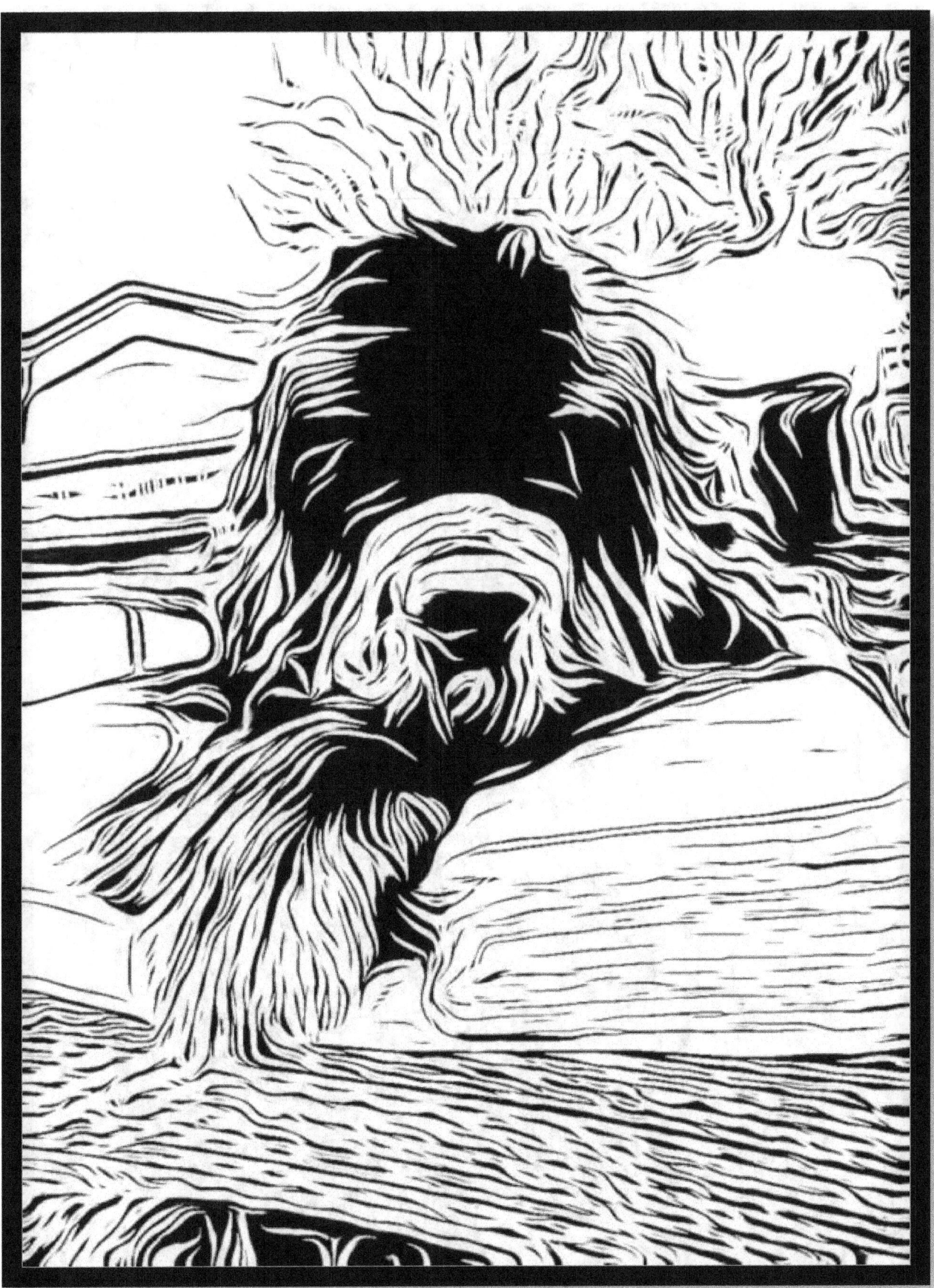

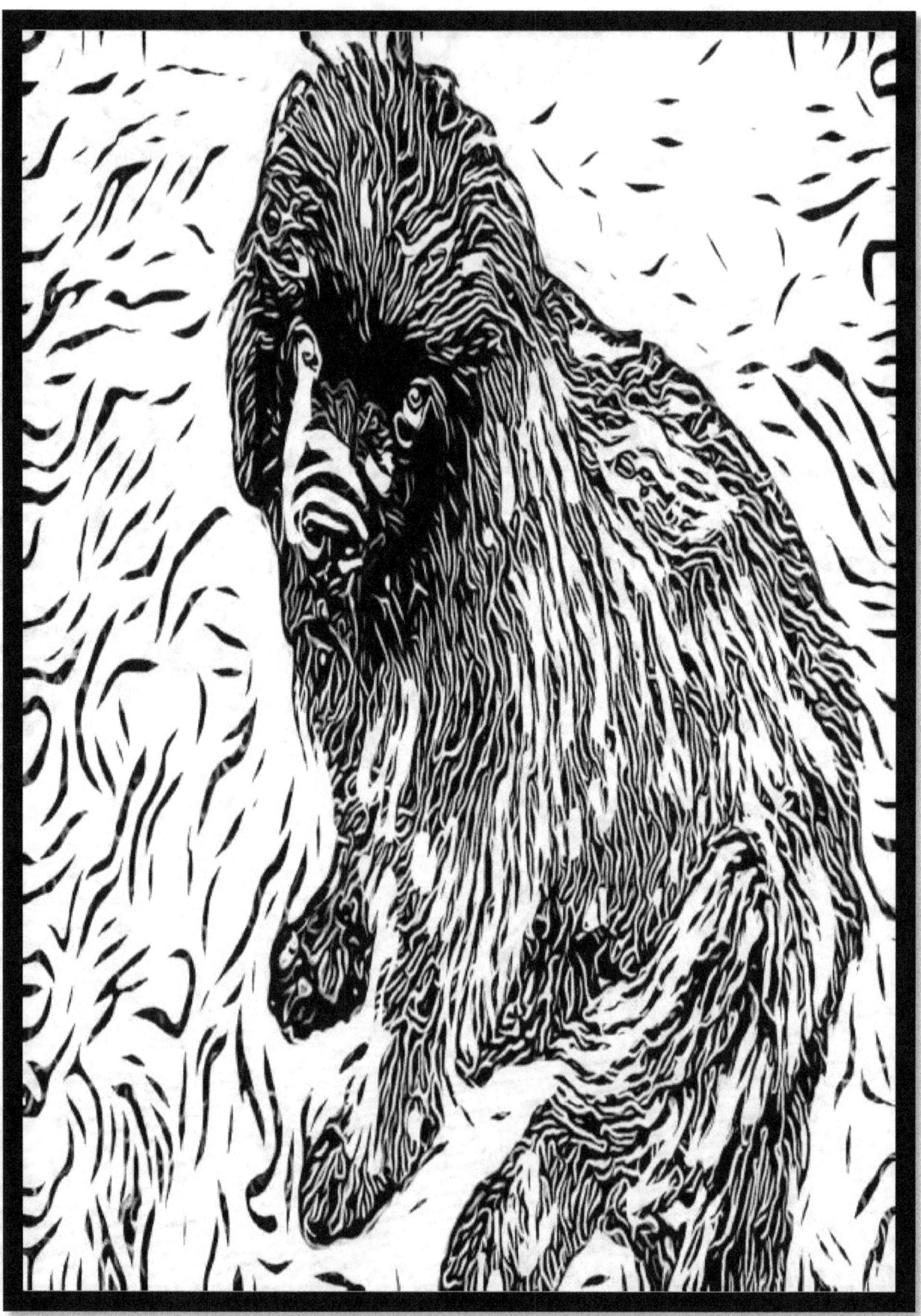

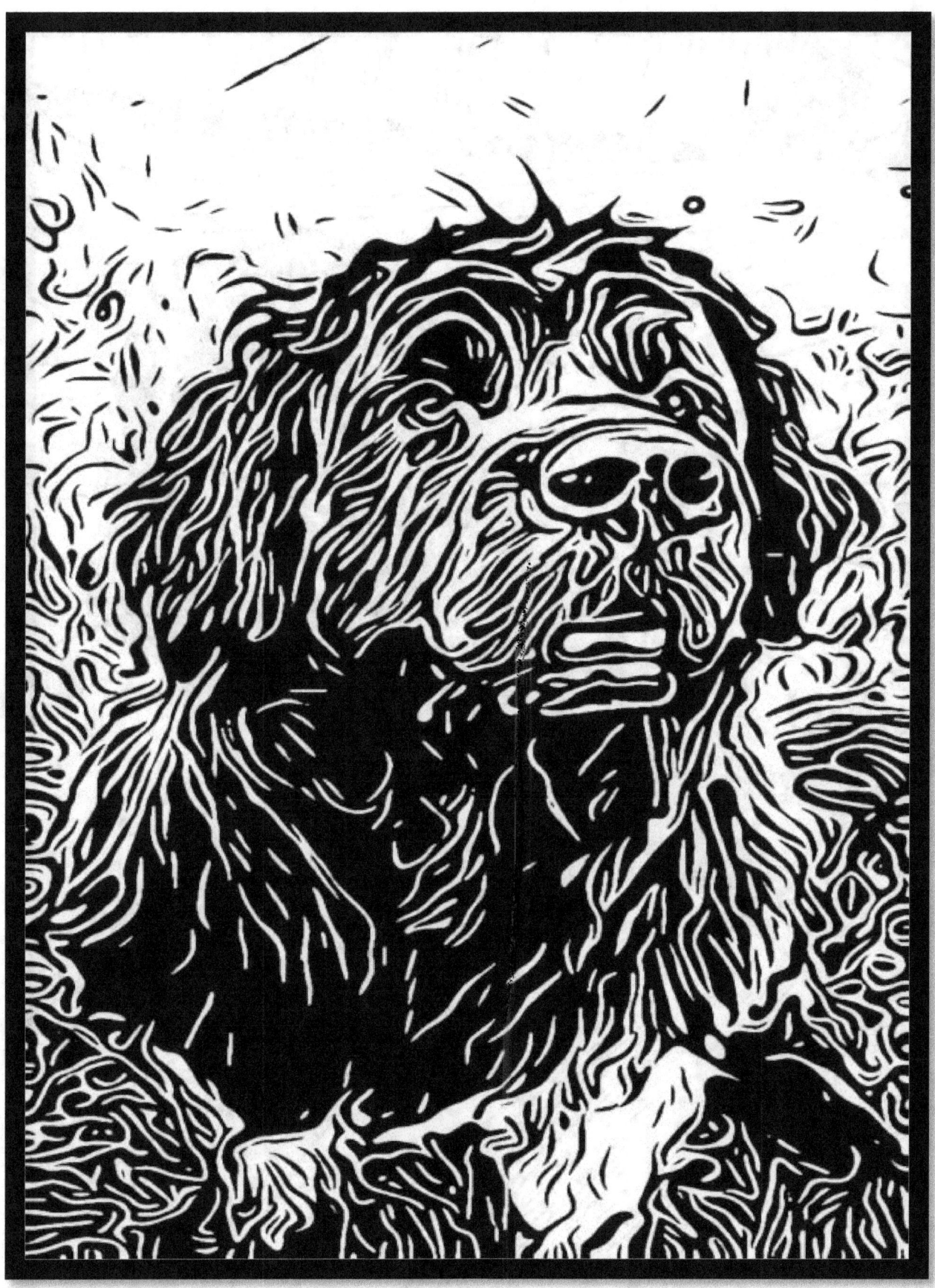

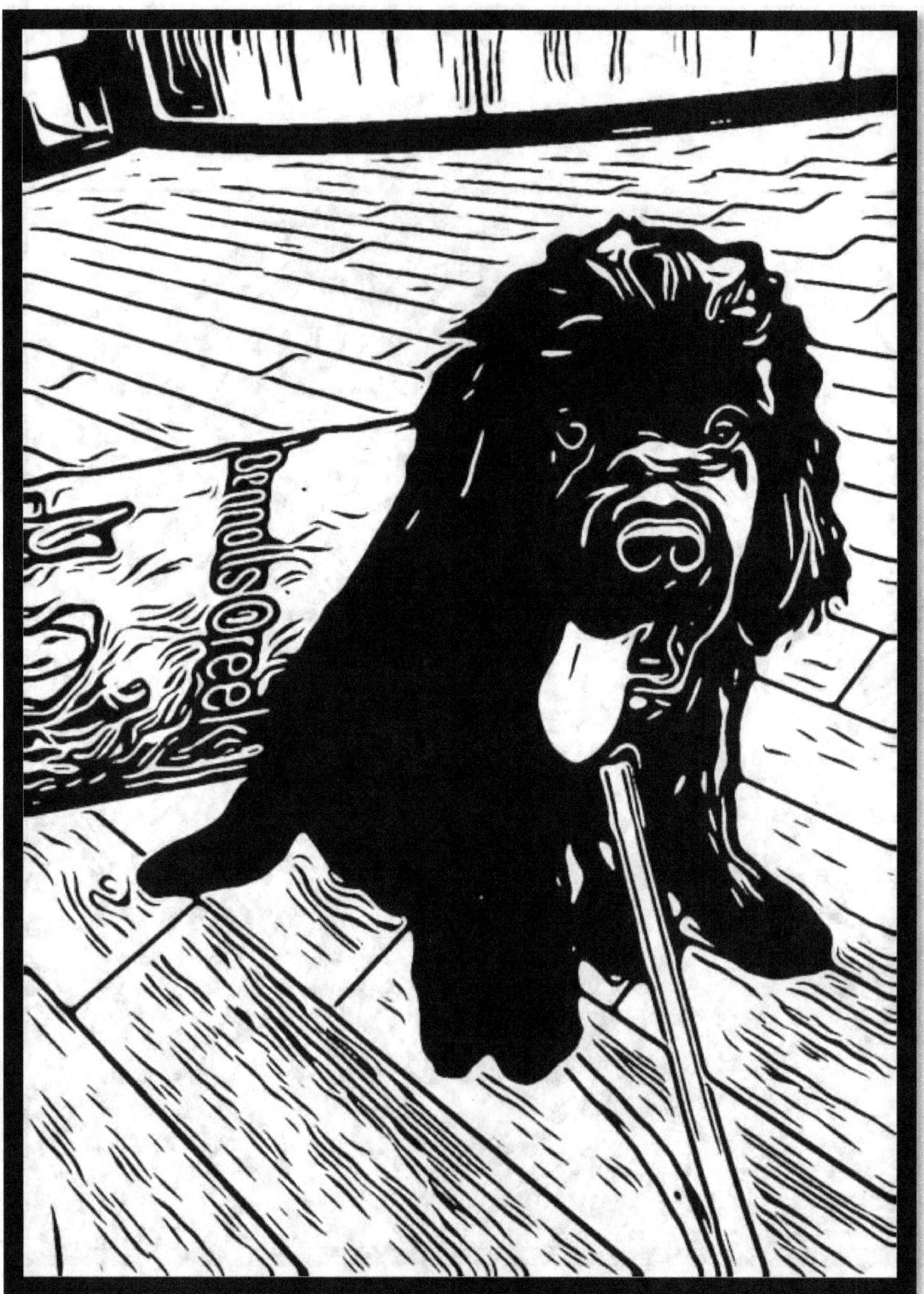

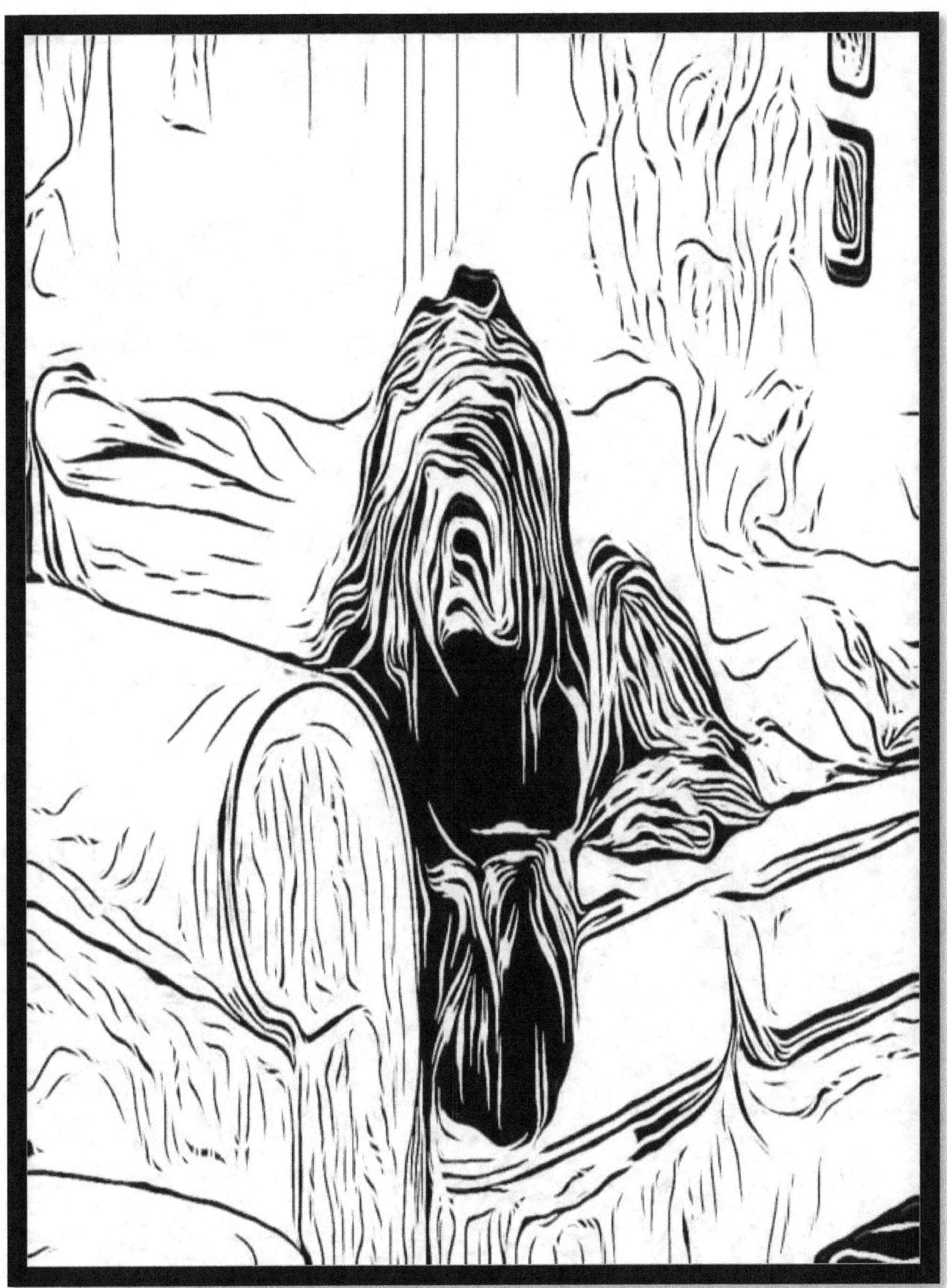

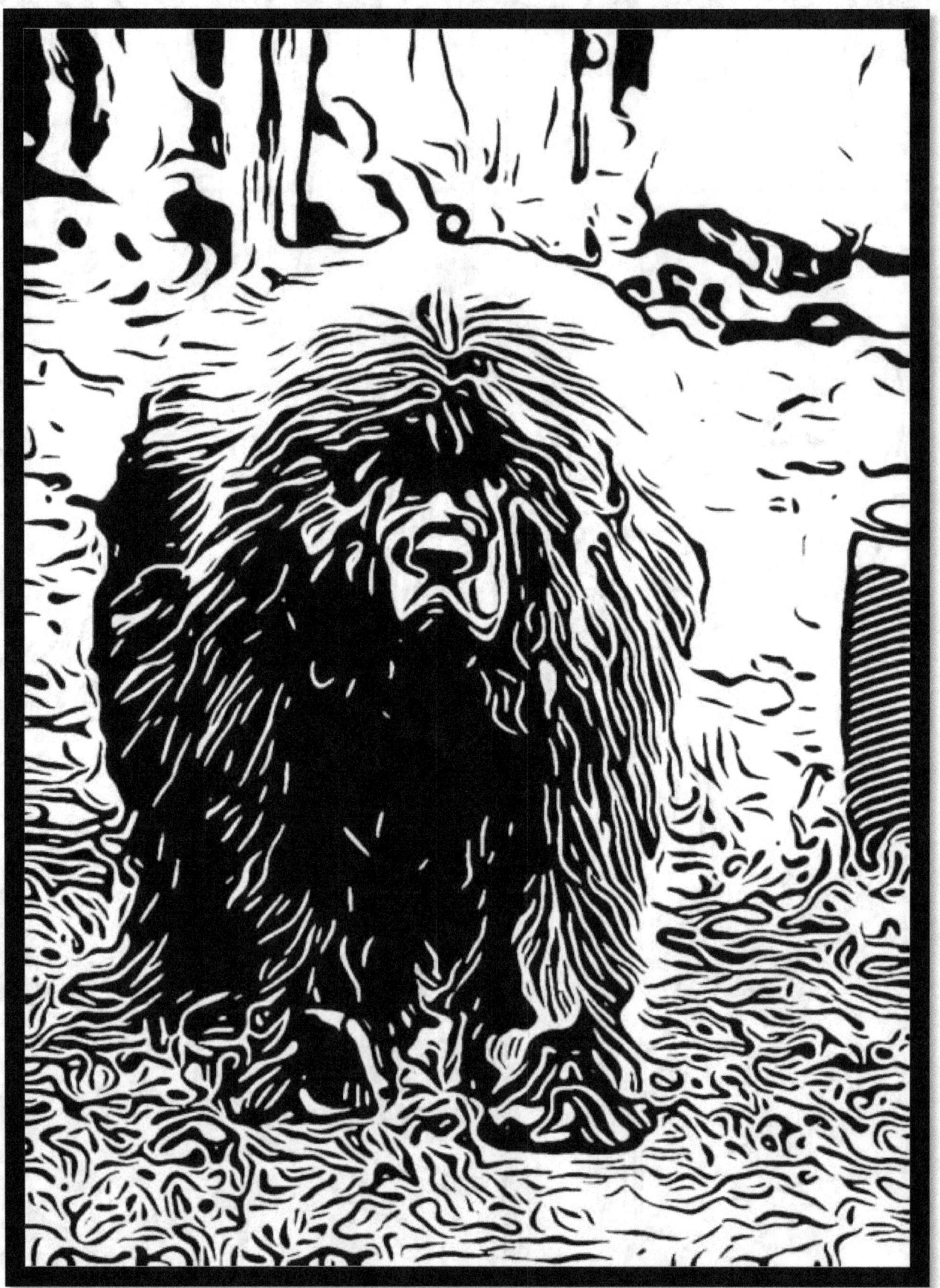

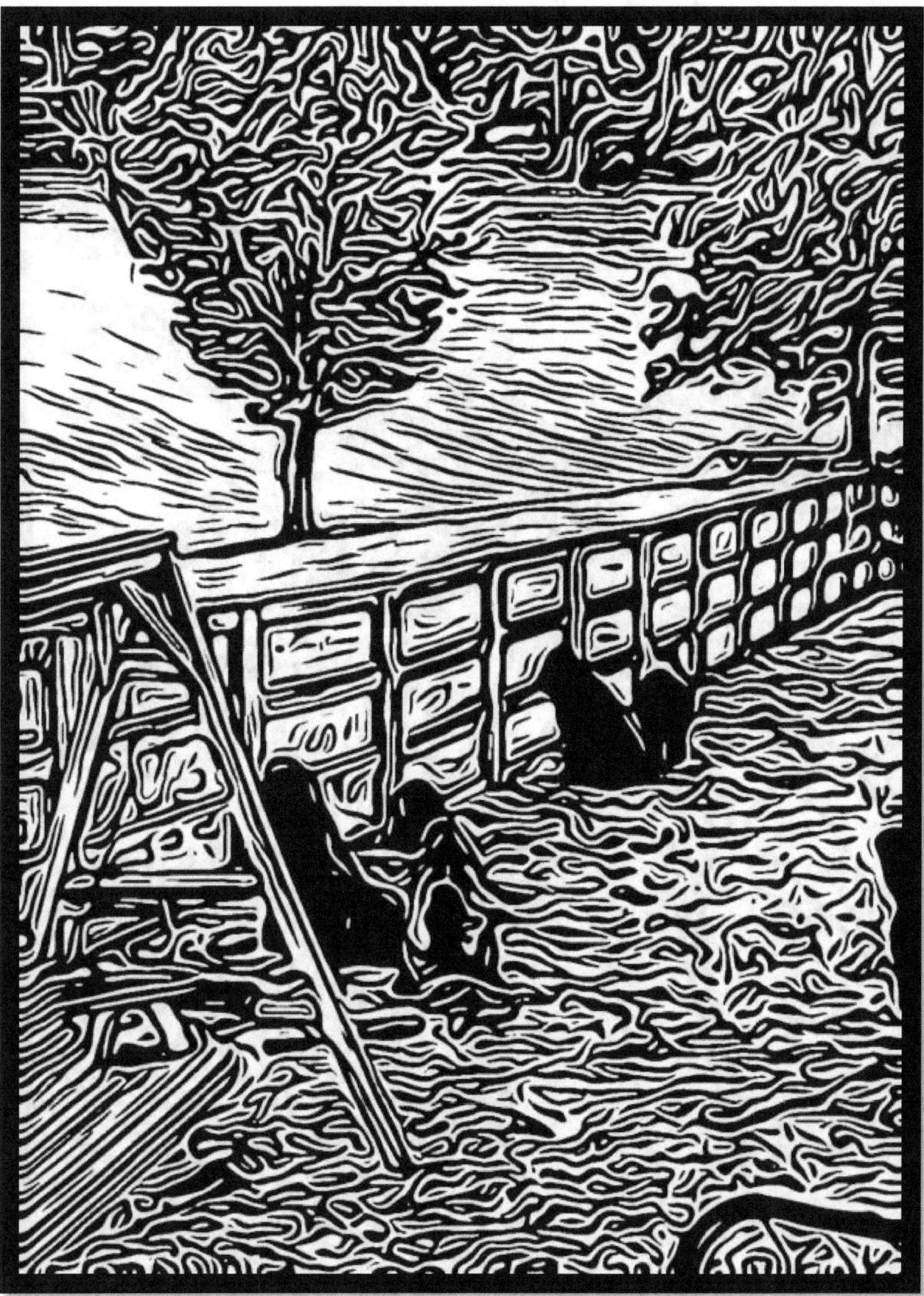

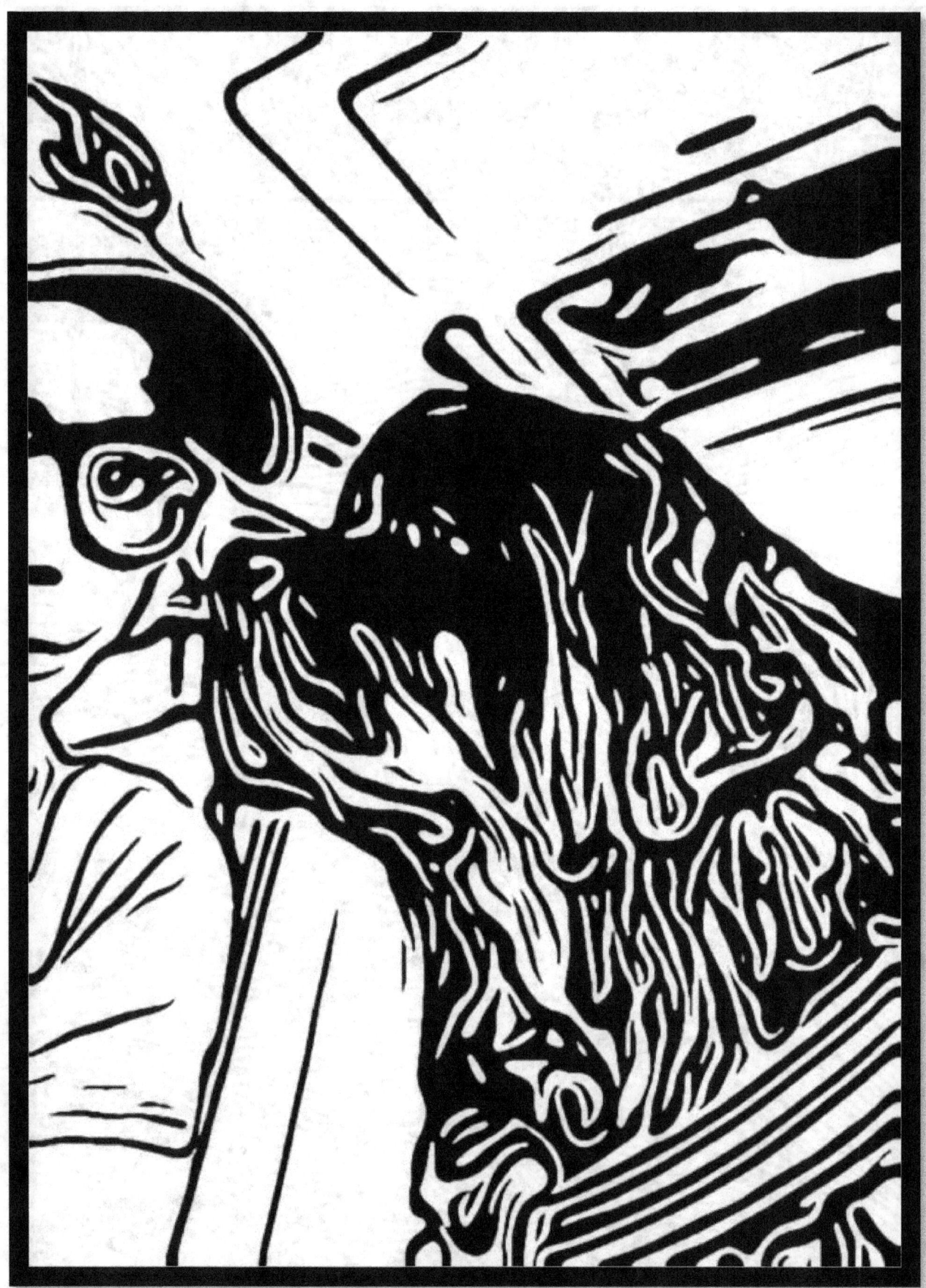

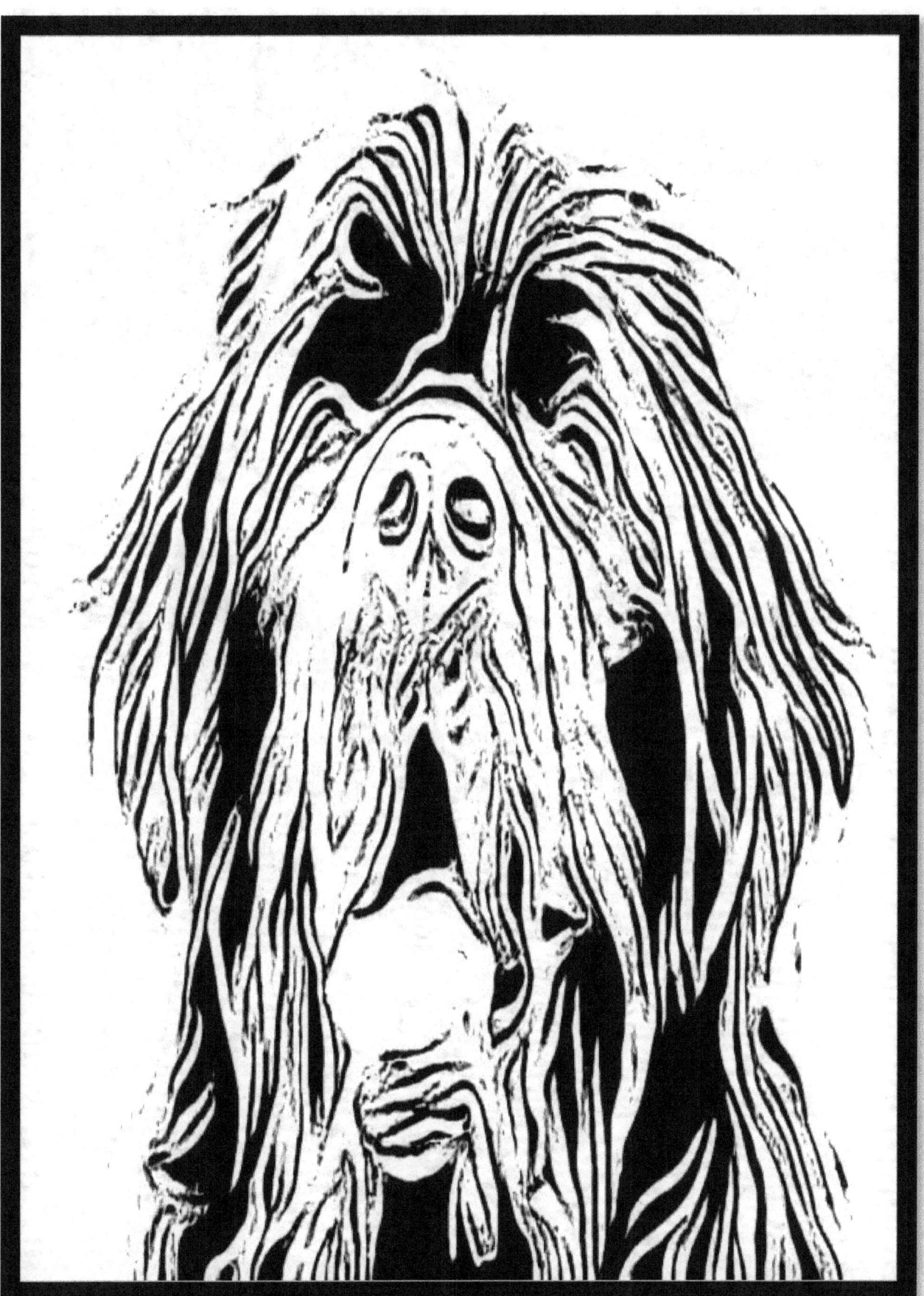

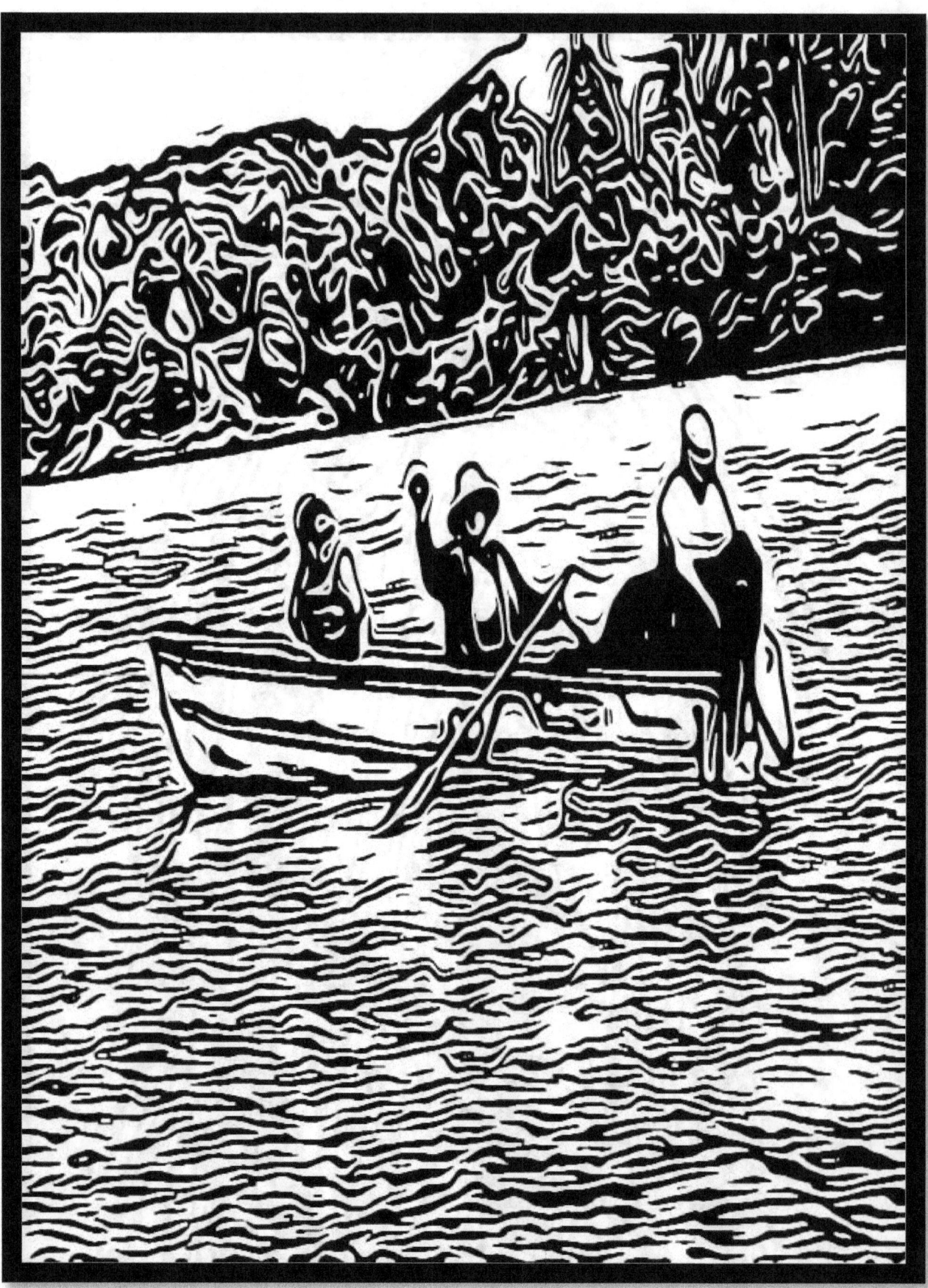

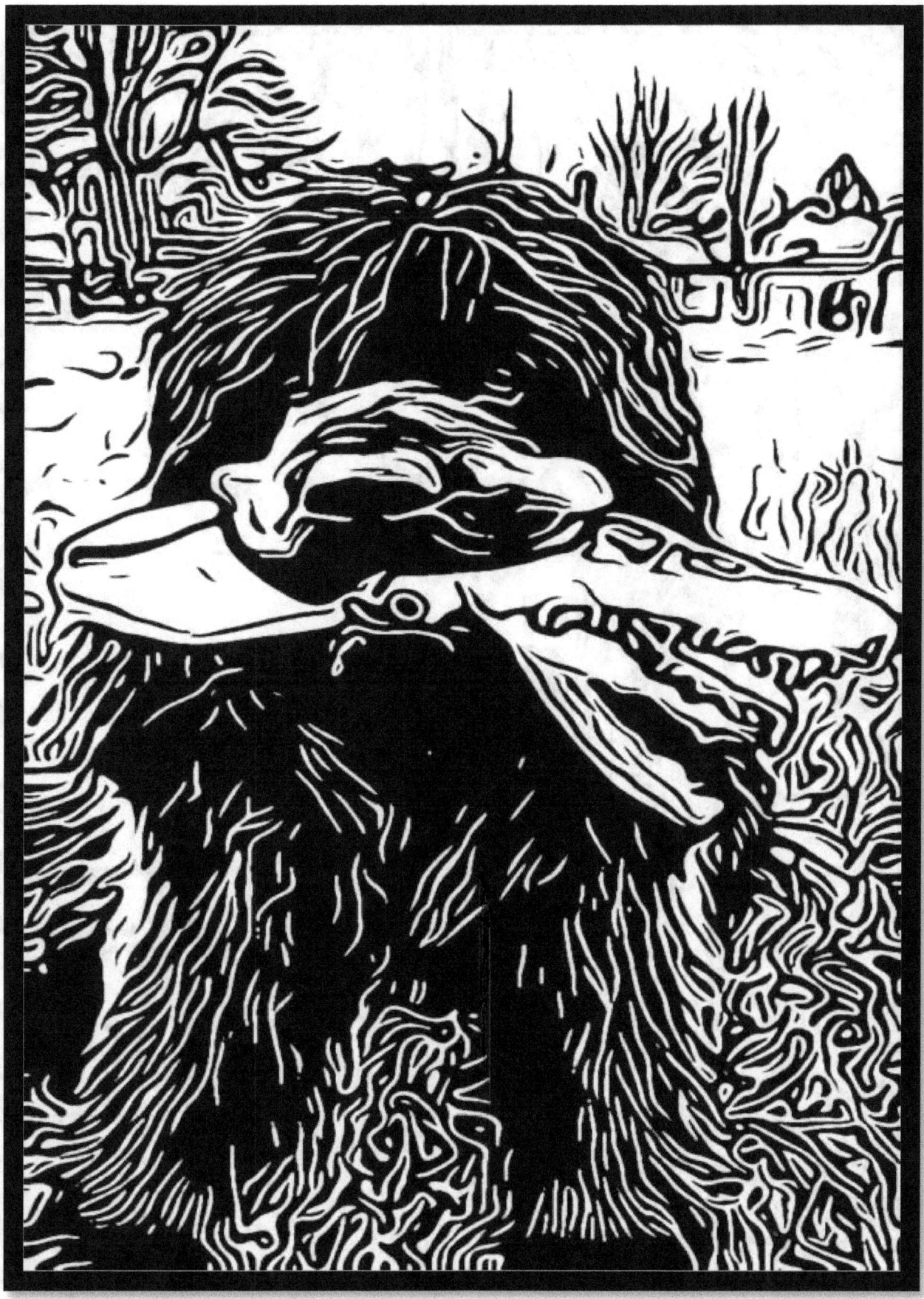

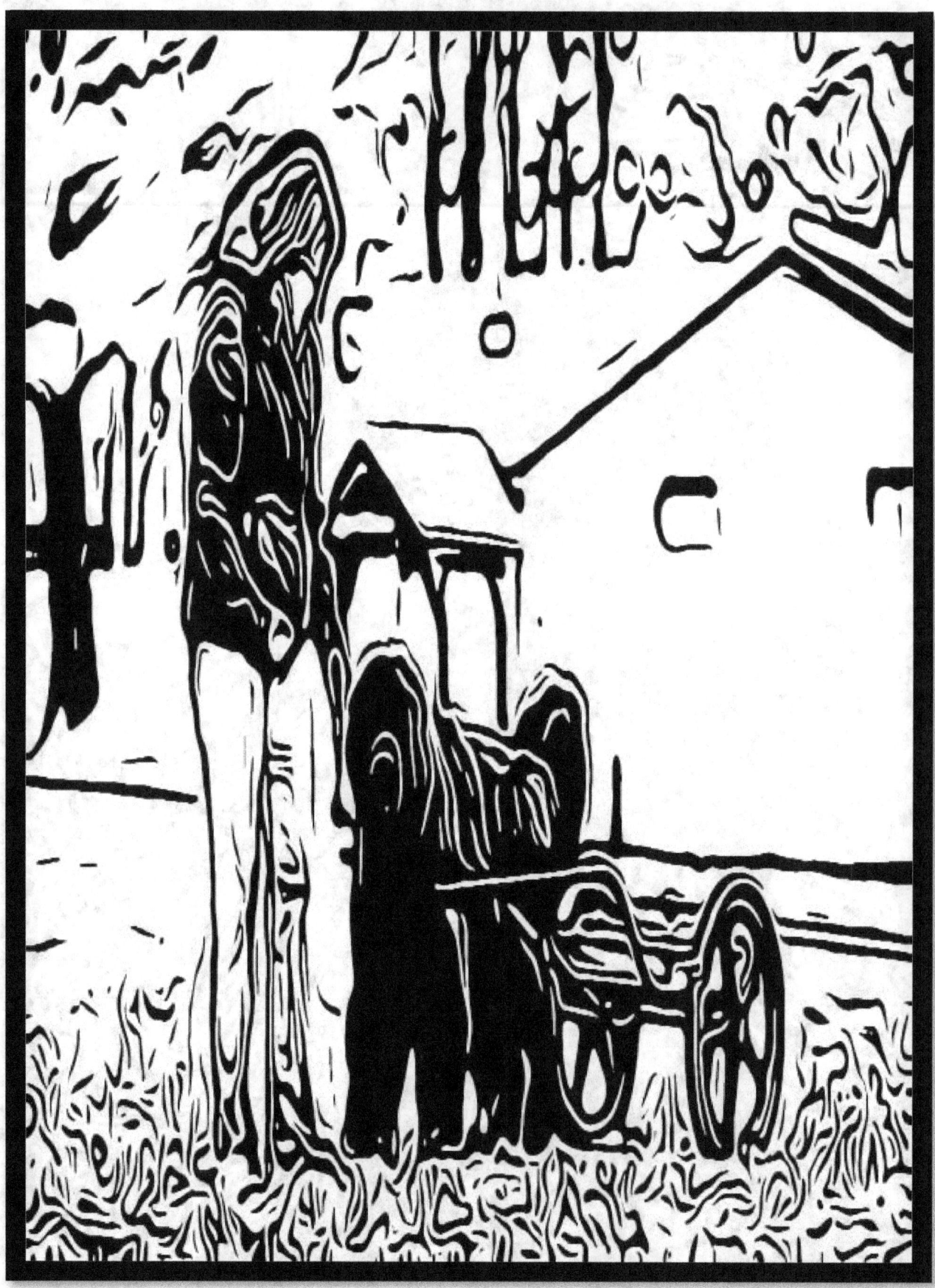

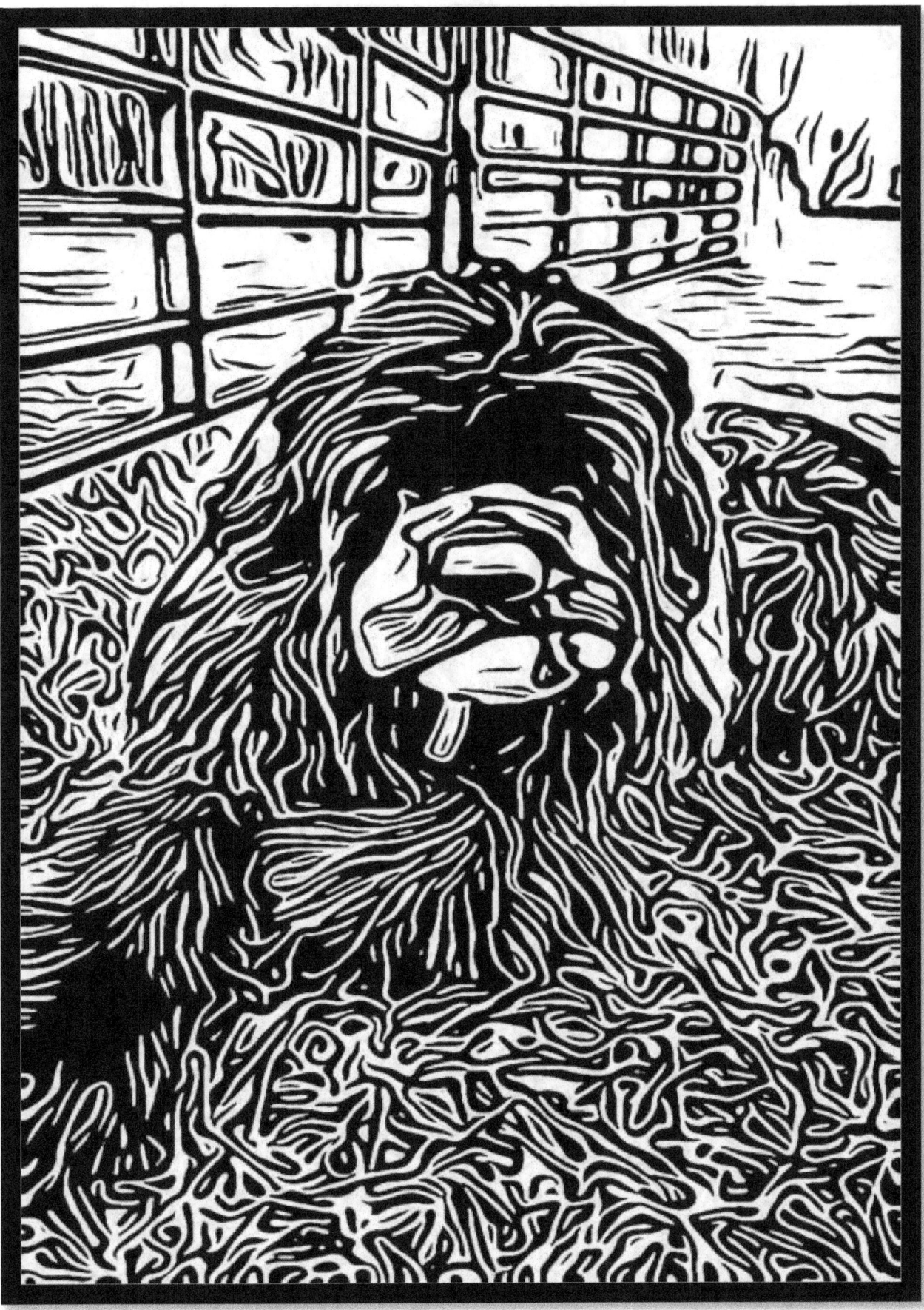

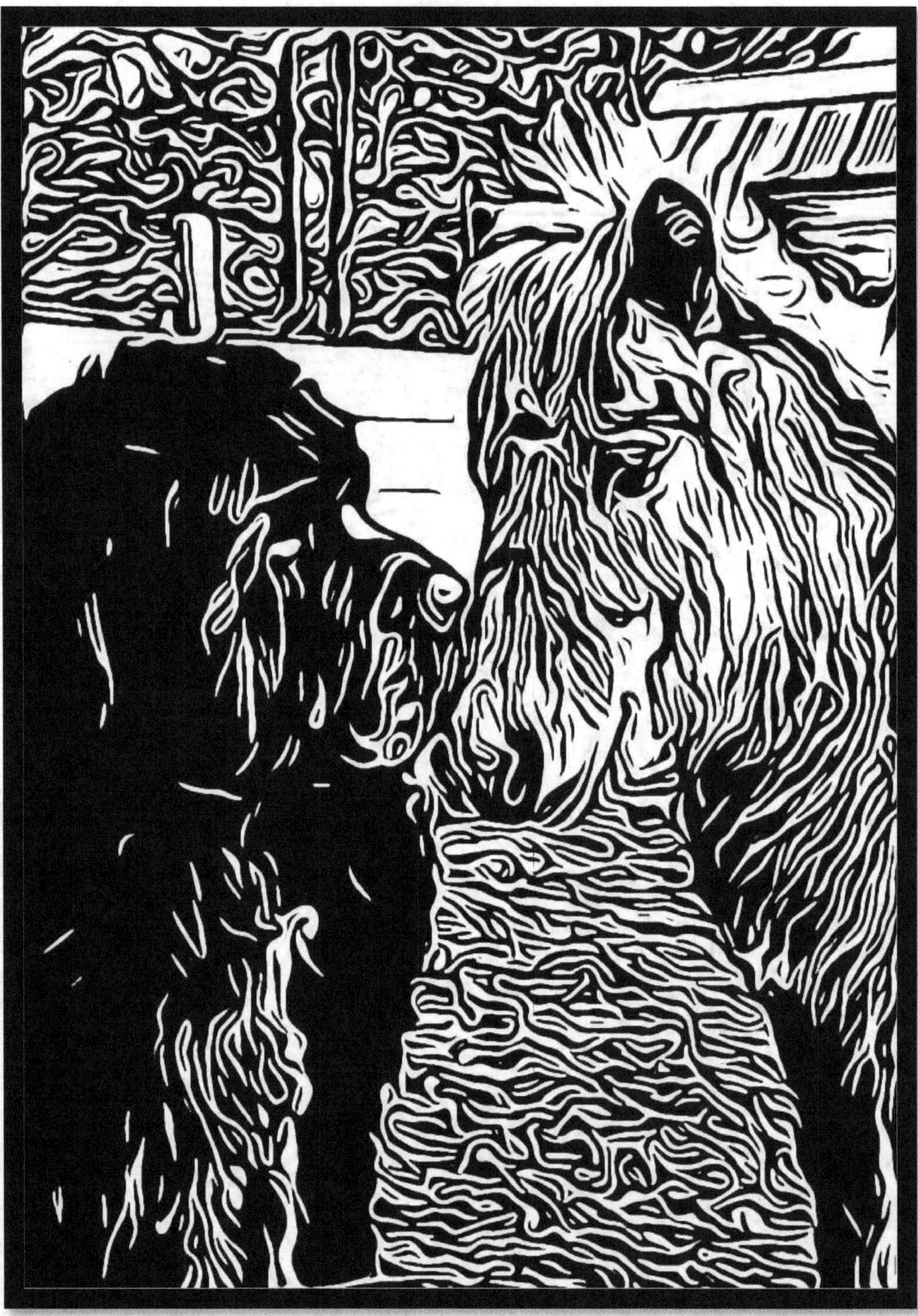

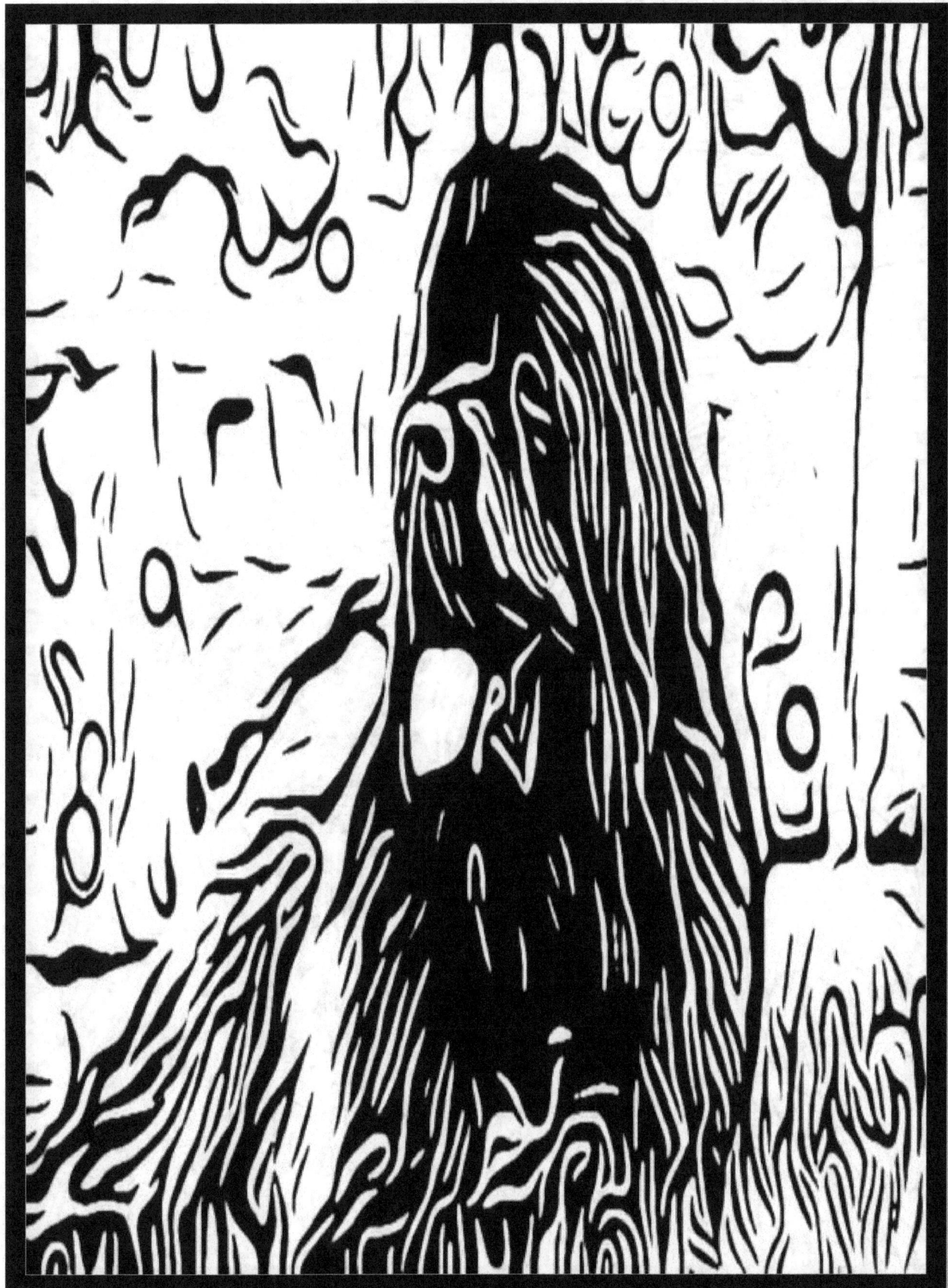

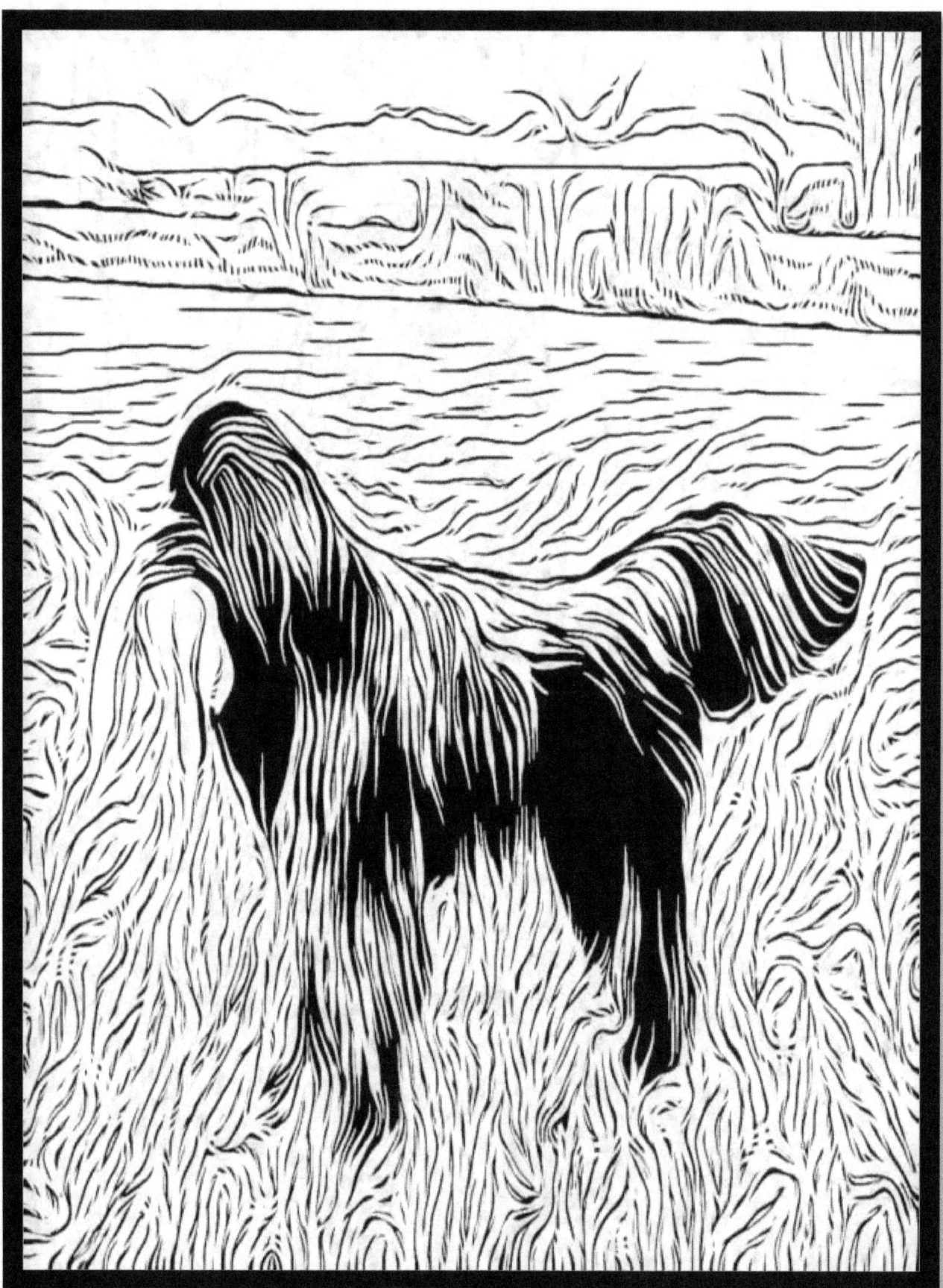

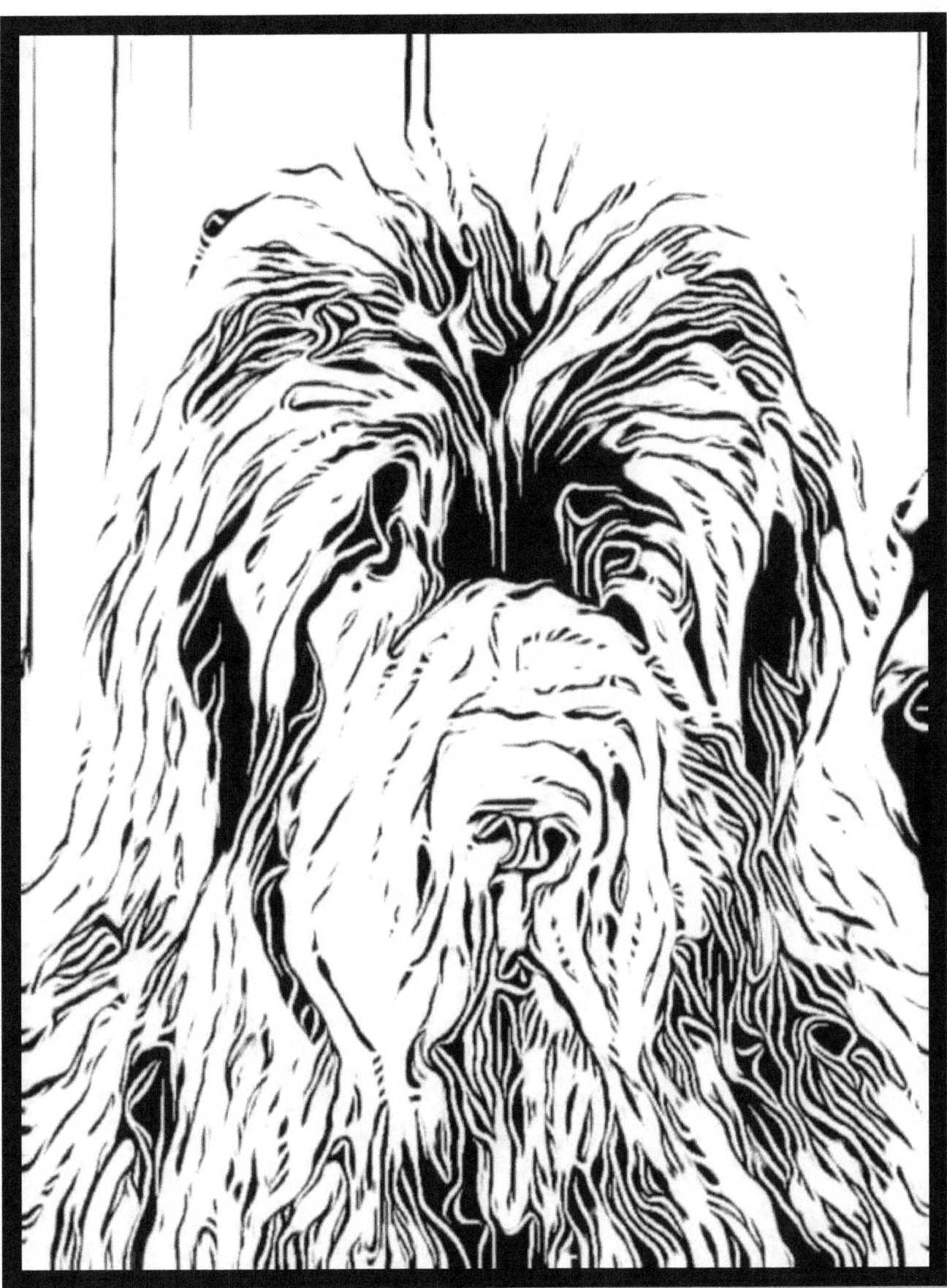

For More Information about:
Newfoundland Dog Pet Therapy
Visit us at:
NewfieTherapy.org
email: info@newfietherapy.org

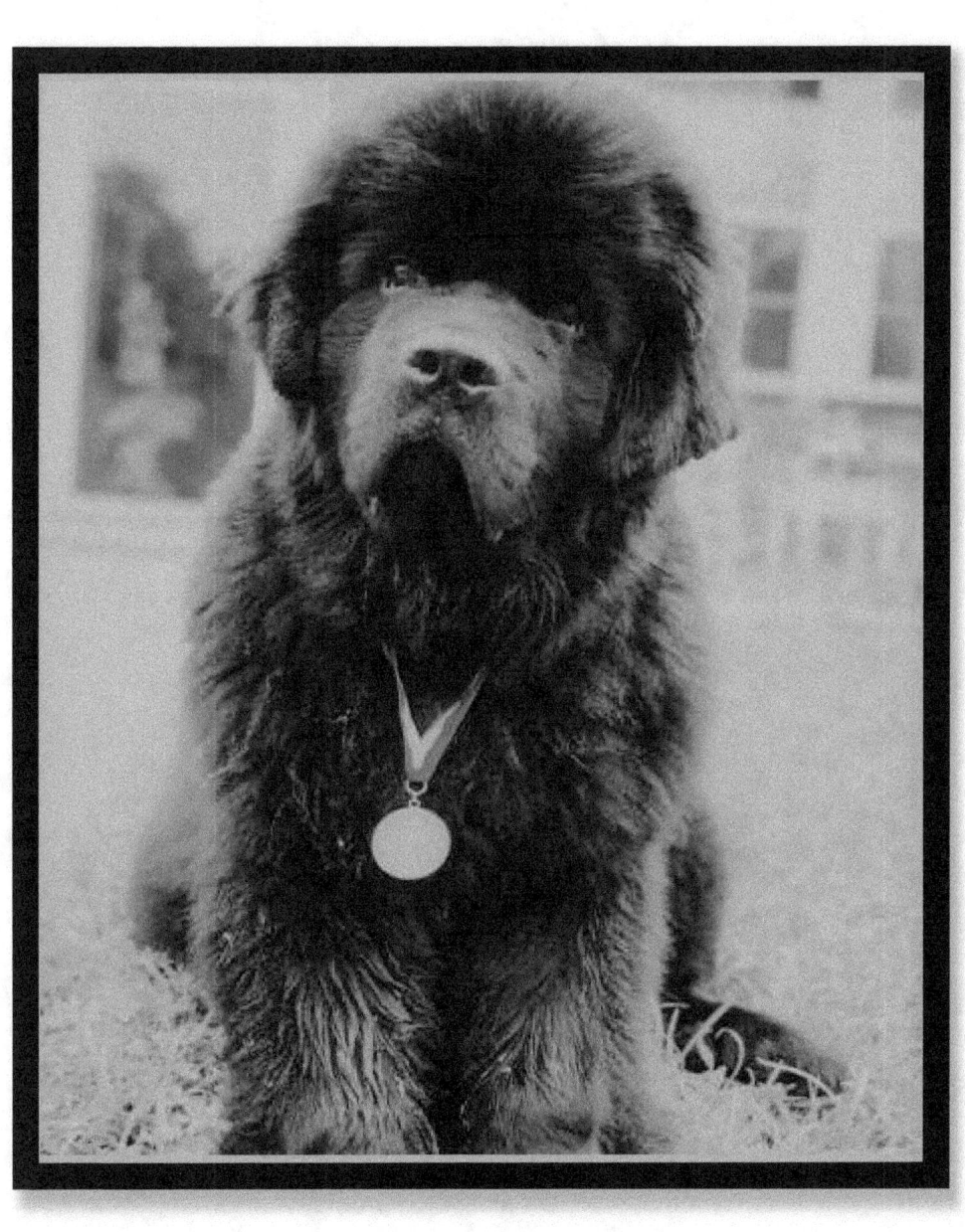

www.ingramcontent.com/pod-product-compliance
Lightning Source LLC
Chambersburg PA
CBHW080442220526
45465CB00007B/2732